With beauty and passion, Elie Wiesel's *Souls on Fire* wove the legends of the Hasidic Masters into "a work," *The New York Times Book Review* praised, "of genius and of art." Now, in *Messengers of God,* Wiesel returns to the sources of his memory, to the legends that enriched his imagination and filled him with wonder and anguish.

Using the interpretation and creative imagination of thousands of years of Jewish history, he retells the timeless stories of those heroes of the Bible who faced their God—and their fellow-men: the stories of Adam and Job and Jacob, of Abraham, Joseph and Moses. He tells the tales of living men and women, not symbols, of human beings possessed of weaknesses, shortcomings, moments of ecstasy and confusion, but thrust into dreams of cosmic magnitude. He shows them to us as they were at the crossroads of their lives: troubled, exalted, marked.

These stories are as much a part of the present as of the past. What is Isaac but the first survivor of a holocaust, Cain and Abel but the first killer and the first victim? In Adam, we see the first creature to discover both the attraction and the danger of secrets and knowledge; in Job, the victim of God and man; in Moses, the leader; in Joseph, the free man, whose efforts transcend the cruelty of his fellow-men.

"All the legends, all the stories retold by the Bible... involve us...Somewhere a father and his son are heading toward an altar in flames; somewhere a dreamy boy knows that his father will die under the veiled gaze of God ... In Jewish history, all events are linked. Only today, after the whirlwind of fire and blood that was the Holocaust, do we grasp the full range of implications of the murder of one man by his brother, the deeper meanings of a father's questions and disconcerting silences. Only as we tell them now, in the light of certain experiences of life and death, do we understand them."

Elie Wiesel's exploration of these events is a rare and masterful job of storytelling, a beautiful transmittal of those stories that are the essence of the Jewish people—and of us all.

Messengers of God is the result of ten years of research, writing and lectures, especially of lectures given at the 92nd Street YM-YWHA in New York.

Messengers
of God

Biblical
Portraits
and Legends

Translated from the French
by Marion Wiesel

NEW YORK

RANDOM HOUSE

Messengers of God

Biblical Portraits and Legends

Elie Wiesel

Library of Congress Cataloging in Publication Data
Wiesel, Elie.
Messengers of God: Biblical portraits
and legends.
Translation of Célébration biblique.
1. Aggada. 2. Midrash—Legends. 3. Tales,
Hasidic. 4. Bible. O. T. Genesis—Legends.
5. Moses—Legends. 6. Job, the patriarch.
I. Title.
BM516.W513   1976   221.9′22 [B]   75-43425
ISBN 0-394-49740-6

Manufactured in the United States of America
2 4 6 8 9 7 5 3
First American Edition

For
Rabbénu Saul Lieberman,
my teacher,
from whom I received more
than, with these pages,
I could ever give back

E.W.

CONTENTS

WHEN I WAS A CHILD, *I read these Biblical tales with a wonder mixed with anguish. I imagined Isaac on the altar and I cried. I saw Joseph, prince of Egypt, and I laughed. Why dwell on them again? And why now? It falls to the storyteller to explain.*

Disciple more than anything else, his aim is not to plunge into historical exegesis—which surely lies beyond his competence—but to reacquaint himself with the distant and haunting figures that molded him. He will try to reconstruct their portraits from Biblical and Midrashic texts, and eventually insert them into the present.

For Jewish history unfolds in the present. Refuting mythology, it affects our life and our role in society. Jupiter is a symbol, but Isaiah is a voice, a conscience. Mars died without ever having lived, but Moses remains a living figure. The calls he issued long ago to a people casting off its bonds reverberate to this day and we are bound by his Law. Were it not for his memory, which encompasses us all, the Jew would not be Jewish, or more precisely, he would have ceased to exist.

Judaism, more than any other tradition, manifests great attachment to its past, jealously keeping it alive. Why? Because we need to. Thanks to Abraham whose gaze is our guide, thanks to Jacob whose dream has us spellbound, our survival, prodigious on so many levels, lacks neither mystery nor significance. If we have the strength and the will to speak out, it is because every one of our forebears expresses himself through us; if the eyes of the world often seem to be upon us, it is because we evoke a time gone by and a fate that transcends time. Panim *in Hebrew is used in the plural form: man has more than one face. His own and Adam's. The Jew is haunted by the beginning more than by the end. His messianic dream is tied to the kingdom of David and he feels closer to the prophet Elijah than to his next-door neighbor.*

What is *a Jew? Sum, synthesis, vessel. Someone who feels every blow that ever struck his ancestors. He is crushed by their mourning and buoyed by their triumphs. For they were living men and women, not symbols. The most pure, the most just among them knew ups and downs, moments of ecstasy and confusion; we know, for they are described to us. Their holiness was defined within human terms of reference. Thus the Jew remembers them and sees them as they were at the crossroads of their own lives: troubled, exalted, marked. They are human beings: people, not gods. Their quest rejoins his own and weighs on his decisions. Jacob's ladder rends his nights. Israel's despair burdens his* solitude. He knows that to speak of Moses is to follow him to Egypt and out of Egypt. To refuse to speak of him is to refuse to follow him.

This is true for all the ancestors and for all their adventures. If Isaac's averted sacrifice had involved only Abraham and his son, their ordeal would have been limited to their own suffering. But it involves us. All the legends, all the stories retold by the Bible and commented on by the Midrash—and here the term Midrash is used in the largest sense: interpretation, illustration, creative imagination— involve us. That of the first killer as well as that of the first victim. We have but to reread them to realize that they are surprisingly topical. Job is our contemporary.

Somewhere a father and his son are heading toward an altar in flames; somewhere a dreamy boy knows that his father will die under the veiled gaze of God. Somewhere a teller of tales remembers, and overcome by an ancient and nameless sadness, he feels like weeping. He has seen Abraham and he has seen Isaac walk toward death; the angel, busy singing the Almighty's praises, did not come to wrest them from the hushed black night.

Everything holds together in Jewish history—the legends as much as the facts. Composed during the centuries that followed the destruction of the Temple in Jerusalem, the Midrash mirrors both the imagined and the lived reality of Israel, and it continues to influence our lives.

In Jewish history, all events are linked. Only today, after the whirlwind of fire and blood that was the Holocaust, do we grasp the full range of implications of the murder of one *man by his brother, the deeper meanings of a father's questions and disconcerting silences. Only as we tell them now, in the light of certain experiences of life and death, do we understand them.*

And so, faithful to his promise, the storyteller does nothing but tell the tale: he transmits what he received, he returns what was entrusted to him. His story does not begin with his own; it is fitted into the memory that is the living tradition of his people.

The legends he brings back are the very ones we are living today.

Messengers
of God

Biblical
Portraits
and Legends

ADAM, OR
THE MYSTERY OF
THE BEGINNING

In THE BEGINNING, man is alone. Alone as God is alone. As he opens his eyes he does not ask: Who am I? He asks: Who are you? In the beginning, man oriented himself solely in relation to God—and all of creation defined itself in relation to man. Before man, things were there, yet did not really exist; under his gaze, they began to be. Before man, time flowed, but it acquired its true dimension only as it penetrated man's consciousness.

Adam: the first being to have a name, to experience joy, surprise and agony; the first man to live both his life and his death; the first creature to discover both the attraction and danger of secrets and knowledge.

To evoke Adam is to evoke the awesome mystery of the beginning, which we are forbidden to do, at least in public. *Ein dorshim maase breshit bishnayim,* says the Talmud. The secret of creation may be dwelled upon only when one is alone—as Adam was alone. It is a subject which tran-

3

scends language and understanding. He who delves into it risks finding himself cut off from the present and remaining isolated and silenced forever.

And yet, Adam is part of us to the extent that man recognizes that he is both point of departure and fulfillment. He knows where he is heading but not whence he comes. Yet he would like to know: the past intrigues him more than death. He is obsessed more by Adam than by the Messiah. Adam frightens him, and his fear resists the most glowing of hopes.

A philosopher once taunted Rabban Gamliel: Your God is indeed a great artist, His Adam was a masterpiece; but you must admit that He had excellent ingredients at His disposal. What were they? asked the sage. The philosopher named some basic elements in nature: fire, wind, dust; and added chaos, the abyss and darkness, without which no work of art is possible.

All these elements are indeed present in Adam's personality, the most complex and colorful in Jewish legend. Adam is impulsive like fire, fickle like the wind and as unpredictable as those romantic characters, bearers of turmoil and eternal remorse, whom only God could console and only God refuses to console.

The Bible devotes no more than a chapter and a half to his life: a few facts, a few encounters with God, the adventure with Eve, exile. His story, in Genesis, is contained in forty verses. His life spanned nine hundred thirty years—

we can survey it in a matter of minutes.

As always, the Midrash tries to compensate for Biblical terseness and offers a portrait both elliptical and striking. Adam: the first living contradiction. Humble yet arrogant, saint and sinner, strong and yet terribly weak. It is for him and because of him that God manifested Himself in creation, and it is because of him and through him that death entered into it as well. One source describes him as having two faces, thus stressing his ambivalence, not to say ambiguity. Why do Scriptures offer us two different versions of Adam's birth? Were there two "first men" at the beginning of history? Or are we to understand that even in the early days of his solitude Adam was already two—as though to warn us that while man aspires to oneness, he will never attain it.

But then we have the right to ask the question: Why such a split, such an explosion of the self, which inevitably must lead to endless conflicts and contradictions? Perhaps God intended to begin His work with a question. Perhaps He sought, through Adam, to continuously interrogate His creation. Therefore, in the beginning, there was neither the word, nor love, but the question which has come to bear God's seal, linking man both to his origins and to his end. Thus the sum of our interrogations reflects the original question, which affected more than Adam, for it did not die with him.

Can we today identify with our first forebear? The Talmud tells us that no man resembles another, yet all men, in every age, resemble Adam: every man recognizes him-

self in him. Our wishes are rooted in his and so are our
sorrows. Our features bear his imprint and so do our
gestures. Condemned to imitate him, we are as he was, we
behave according to his example. There is but one difference: we have a past, whereas he had none. No memory
preceded his own. Born an adult, thrust into a pre-
arranged universe, he was denied the possibility of escap-
ing into childhood dreams or adolescent preoccupations.
There was no way out of the present, no refuge in fantasy.
The most wretched, the most destitute of mortals comes
from somewhere—not Adam. The poorest of men possesses memories torn from yesterday's world, longings,
vantage points—not Adam. To correct this injustice, God
gave him . . . a future, the longest in the history of mankind. And He allowed Adam to see it in its totality, to the
very last generation: their judges and their kings, their
sages and their thieves, their profiteers and their prophets.
Thus the first man beheld the image of the last of his
descendants and their eyes met. More than the Messiah,
Adam is present.

The man who emerges from the various texts and commentaries is appealing and we take him to our hearts. His
problems are ours, we are distressed over his fate, his
tense, troubled, inexplicably threatened home. We would
like to help him. His every move concerns us, we share his
fears, his disappointments. Nobody received as much and
nobody lost it as quickly or as brutally. Nor was he to

blame in any way. He was pushed and was helpless to resist. No one asked him anything; he was made to obey a will other than his own. Everything belonged to him except his will. He had no choice but to submit. First to God, then to his spouse. Traps were laid for him and he fell into them. Poor man: punished for nothing. And he wasn't even Jewish.

Embodying man's eternal quest for meaning, justice and truth, Adam remains the contemporary—and the companion—of all men, of all generations. Every one of us yearns to recapture some lost paradise, every one of us bears the mark of some violated, stolen innocence. All our passions and sorrows, all our failings, Adam already knew. He had to contend with all our inhibitions, manias and complexes, with one exception: the Oedipus complex, thank heaven.

We learn all this from Talmudic literature. Adam's life is presented there as a tragedy in three acts, with the entire universe as stage and setting. As if to underline the allegorical dimension of the main character, the Midrash inserts him into the condensed time associated with classical theater. Born at the age of forty, his tragedy lasts only one day.

Listen to the Midrash: It was in the first hour of the sixth day that God conceived the project of creating man. In the second hour He consulted the angels—who opposed the project—and the Torah—which approved. In the third hour God selected the clay for Adam's body. In the fourth hour He gave it shape. In the fifth hour He covered it with skin. In the sixth hour He completed the body and made it stand up. In the seventh hour He breathed a soul into it. In the eighth hour Adam was ushered into paradise. In the ninth hour he heard the divine commandment forbidding him to eat from the Tree of Knowledge. In the tenth hour he transgressed. In the eleventh hour he was judged by a seventy-one-member Sanhedrin. And in the twelfth hour of the sixth day he was found guilty and expelled from paradise.

Thus ends Adam's story, and thus begins the story of mankind. Born to affirm God's glory, Adam became the incarnation of His first defeat.

No wonder God had His doubts about the project. He was not convinced that it was a good idea to place man at the center of His universe. He looked into the future and saw that there were among Adam's descendants innumerable sinners thirsting for crime and blood. Yet He also foresaw that side by side with them, there would be saints and Just Men. So, for the joy of blessing the chosen, God consented to let Himself be afflicted with the wicked.

One Midrash tells us that when He made His decision, God disregarded the advice of two of His angels whose common sense led them to urge prudence. Said the Angel of Truth: What good is it to create man? Surely he will be a liar. And the Angel of Peace added: In what way does he deserve to be given life? Surely he will provoke endless wars. Yet the Angels of Justice and Mercy pronounced themselves favorably: Let man be born and he will be just and merciful. God—we are told—did away with the rebellious angels, destroying them by fire. Another, less radical, version recounts that while the angels were quarreling among themselves, God took advantage of their inattention and hastily created man.

And He created him in His image . . .

So much so that, according to Rabbi Shmuel Bar-Nahman, centuries later while Moses was transcribing the Torah, he stopped at this passage and questioned God: Master of the Universe, aren't You concerned that with these words You may give comfort to the miscreants and mislead the innocent and the naïve? If it is true that God created man in His image, will it not be said then that God has an image? And that therefore God is not one, but many? God reassured His servant: You, Moses, son of Amram, write—that is your task and your role. As for those who will refuse to understand or who will deliberately misinterpret My thoughts and yours, well, let that be their problem.

Evidently Moses mistrusted the close relationship that had existed between God and Adam. Rabbinical tradition reduces this danger to a minimum, striving to link Adam to man—to all men.

A Midrash: Why did God create one man and not more? To give us a lesson in equality and teach us that no man is superior to another; we all have the same forebear. That is also why the clay from which he was fashioned was gathered from every corner of the universe; thus no one can claim that the world or Adam belongs to him alone. Adam belongs to all men and to each to the same degree.

Also, so that a just man could not say: I am the son of

a just man. And a non-believer: I am the son of a non-believer. And so that one man could not taunt another, saying: My father was greater than yours. And so that every man would feel responsible for the entire world. Since the world was created for one human being, whoever kills one human being, kills all mankind; and whoever saves one human being, saves all mankind. One text offers this cynical explanation: God created one single individual in order to prevent quarrels. And the text continues: Nonetheless, in spite of this precaution, men go on quarreling and killing one another. Imagine what would have happened to the world if God, in the beginning, had created more than one man?

Another question: Why did the Creator wait until the sixth day to give life to Adam—why didn't he do it at the very start? Answer: When a king invites a guest, he first prepares a palace for him and only then asks him to come. Man is creation's guest of honor. Another answer: To keep man from taking himself too seriously, from growing vain or arrogant, he could be asked: What are you boasting about—even mosquitoes preceded you in the order of creation?

And yet the Midrash attributes so many talents and virtues to Adam that it is difficult to understand how he did not fall victim to pride. In this respect, Jewish legend differs from most secular concepts, which consider the human being a function of progress. Never mind Darwin and his theory of evolution. Never mind Schopenhauer, who called man a "crazy wild beast restrained only by civilisation." According to him, the further back one goes, the deeper one delves into the past, the more man emerges as a primitive creature dominated by obscure, irrational and deadly instincts.

In Jewish tradition it is just the opposite: man's past is linked to history's sacred origins. A divine reflection, the first man was more righteous, more accomplished than the most "evolved" of his descendants would ever be.

What has not been said about Adam? He was so tall that his body spanned the earth from one end to the other. And so beautiful that the splendor of his heel outshone that of the sun. And so powerful that the wild beasts trembled in his presence.

To illustrate Samson's strength, the Midrash compares it to that of Adam. The same comparison is drawn for Absalom's hair, Assa's legs and Zidkiyahu's eyes. Adam: the prototype of perfect man. The ideal mold. The supreme example.

Wise, intelligent, erudite, understanding, generous, he was endowed with a flawless soul. Incapable of wrongdoing, of thinking ill; closed to weakness, to doubts. Moreover, he was humble, shy, grateful. Some sources refer to him as *Hasid.* Others call him the luminary, the "candle of the world." Some go as far as seeing in him the future Messiah. So glorious was he that the angels, dazzled by his perfection, confused him with his Creator and began to sing him their praises. God responded by making him fall asleep and the frightened angels recognized their error. (As for me, I'd rather think that Adam fell asleep not because of God but because of the angels: nothing bores a perfect man more than excessive praise.)

For Adam was indeed bored in paradise; all the texts point to it. Since he had the whole universe to himself, he desired nothing, thought of nothing and nobody. Happy, content, he seems singularly uninteresting before his downfall. No cloud, no shadow to mar his serenity. His indifference to the world extended to his own person. No trace of foreboding or concern. He was intoxicated with God, brimming over with God, joined to God in God: no need for him to seek God, to serve Him, understand Him, woo Him. So total was God's presence, he did not feel it. Nor did he think of it; he didn't need to, for the very source and cradle of his mind were occupied by God.

One pictures his life as drab, devoid of expectation, of stimulation. Like God, Adam was surrounded by angels acting as servants. One prepared his meals, another tasted his wines. From time to time God invited him to join Him in His walks and showed him the visible and hidden beauties of nature: Look well, Adam, all this immensity was created for your sake alone; be careful, do not destroy anything, for after you there will be no one to repair what you have undone. A superfluous warning, for Adam had no thought of destroying or even of changing anything. He was content; he accepted everything, himself included.

No wonder Satan grew jealous. In those days Satan was not just anybody. He was an influential angel, God's favorite, and he was seated at His right. God was amused by his imagination and forgave him his whims and escapades. Thus Satan couldn't but resent the intruder who was succeeding too easily and too quickly; he *had* to fight the newcomer, he *had* to undermine his position. How? He gossiped, intrigued, plotted; he spared no means.

To disarm Satan and bring him back to reason, God decided to prove to him that Adam was the more intelligent of the two, and thus worthy of his success. All the animals on earth were summoned to appear before Him. Would you know how to name them? God asked Satan. No, he would not. And you, Adam? Adam named them all; and to name things is to possess them. And to God's satisfaction, he was declared the winner. One Midrashic text insinuates that God cheated. Wanting to assure Adam's victory, He asked the questions in such a way that Adam could guess the answers; he couldn't possibly lose. Is that to say that without help Adam would have failed the test? No. The last question is proof. God chose not to whisper the answer when He asked: And Me, Adam, what name will you give Me? Adam rose to the challenge. He cast aside his humility and called God by His name. He understood intuitively that God Himself receives His name from man—illustrating the basic Jewish concept that while God is God and man is only His instrument, still God needs man to make Himself known, just as man needs God to acquire this knowledge.

Having reached this point in the story, we must pause, for its setting is changing: Adam is about to leave his fairy tale to enter tragedy.

And since no tragedy seems convincing or even quite possible without a woman in the cast, both Bible and Talmud call upon Eve to enter the action.

Needless to say, she immediately tried to eclipse her only partner—and succeeded. From the moment she appeared, she took over center stage. She entered Adam's life and dominated it completely. We see and hear only her. In no time, Adam became the prototype of the weak, submissive husband whose passivity turns into an act of sheer survival. Unbelievable but true: the very man God considered His masterpiece, His crowning achievement, turned into a pallid figure content to follow his wife and let her decide for him, for both. He could not say no to her; he submitted and kept silent.

Why was Eve created? For Adam's sake, of course. That is what he was told repeatedly. She was to help him by opposing him, by defying him; she was to enrich his life and lead him to discover desire, ambition and remorse. Eve: a remedy against solitude, the unfathomed side of man. Without Eve, Adam would have been a man but not human.

One Midrashic text candidly admits that Eve was created more to serve God than Adam. God wished this marriage to take place so as to forestall Adam's being looked upon as a divinity, a god on earth just as the Creator is God in heaven. Solitary men are distrusted everywhere, even in heaven. No divine attribute seems as enviable as solitude.

Another text tries to make us believe that it was Adam

who *chose* Eve to be his wife. Could he have taken another? Was there another? Yes, Eve was not the first woman in creation; she had been preceded by Lilith, mother of demons, but Adam didn't love her, couldn't love her, for he had been present at her creation. She therefore held no mystery, no attraction. And so God introduced Eve, and Adam found her to his liking. Indeed, it was love at first sight.

But why did God take her from her future husband's rib? The question evidently did not trouble Adam, but seems to have preoccupied the Midrash, which offers the following explanation. Before carrying out His project, God thought to Himself: I shall not take her from Adam's head, for then she might carry her head too high, flaunting her arrogance and pride; nor shall I take her from his eyes, for then she might tend to be curious, too curious and greedy; nor must I take her from his ears, for she might tend to eavesdrop; nor from his neck, for she might be stiff-necked and insolent; nor from his mouth, for she would not stop chattering; nor from his heart, for she would be sick with jealousy; nor from his hand, for she might turn into a meddler. No, God decided, I shall take her from the most chaste part of Adam's body—his rib. And, adds the Midrash with caustic humor, despite these precautions, woman has all the faults God tried to prevent.

But before we accuse the Midrash of anti-feminist tendencies, let us listen to another, more flattering, text:

A king met Rabban Gamliel and told him: I don't know

how to say this, but . . . your God—yes, your God—is nothing but a thief. Here was Adam sleeping the sleep of the just and suddenly God steals one of his ribs. —Rabban Gamliel's daughter chose to answer the sovereign: Do you know what happened to me last night, Your Majesty? Thieves entered my house; they took all my silver and in its place they left me gold. — If only I could be the victim of such robbers every night, said the king. — Well, said the sage's daughter, that is precisely what happened to Adam. True, God did take a rib from him, but in exchange he gave him a beautiful woman who helped him when he needed help, served him when he needed to be served and was silent when he talked.

But why wasn't Adam consulted first? After all, it was a matter of some concern to him. If indeed there is an answer, I have been unable to find it in our legends. Perhaps God was simply unwilling to risk a refusal.

At any rate, faced with a *fait accompli,* Adam declared himself pleased and ready to comply. Whereupon the marriage was arranged: God officiated and the angels and seraphim took over both the technical and the artistic aspect of the ceremony. There was singing and dancing and joy in every sphere and celestial palace. Never since has a wedding been performed with such pomp or in the presence of such distinguished guests.

The bride and groom might have lived happily ever after, had it not been for the irruption on stage of a new character ushering in the second act.

With the arrival of the serpent, the action changes course. The plot thickens and the reader is caught up in the growing excitement. For the first time the couple faced a third presence. Something was bound to happen. Either Adam and Eve would become closer to one another than ever before or drift apart. Confronted with the serpent, they had to—and were able to—choose. They were in a situation of conflict; they were free—human at last.

The mechanism had been set much earlier. Remember? God had given Adam and Eve full freedom to roam through paradise, doing whatever they liked, eating whatever appealed to them, with one exception: they were not to taste the fruit from the Tree of Knowledge. God had warned them firmly: transgression would result in death. Neither husband nor wife could possibly know what it meant to die, yet they obeyed. And they would have obeyed to the end had not the serpent intervened. He altered the existing rules, and thereafter Adam and Eve were no longer the same.

A strange character, the serpent. Evil and cursed, mythical yet real. His role? One source assures us he was the angels' emissary; they had concluded that man would represent too formidable a challenge unless he could be made to stray and sin. In those days the serpent walked and talked, he even talked quite well. He knew how to convince and get others to obey; he was king of the beasts. A gambler, and vain at that, he was easily persuaded to conspire against those humans, those potential rivals, who were eluding his authority.

1 7

Other sources deny the angels' role in the conspiracy. They claim the initiative came from the serpent himself. He fell in love with Eve and planned to kill Adam and marry his widow. Better yet: to arrange for God to kill Adam, then to abscond with Eve and her fortune—with the heiress and her inheritance. He aimed too high, a legend tells us, and he was punished; he obtained nothing of what he coveted and lost everything he could call his own. God told him: No longer will you reign over the animals; rather, from now on your fate will be lowlier than theirs; no longer will you walk erect or run; from now on you will crawl in the dust.

Whatever the serpent's motivation may have been, one fact remains: his first target was Eve. Why? Rightly or wrongly, he assessed the woman as being more vulnerable, more gullible, more malleable than her husband. He expected that of the two, she would offer the least resistance. His intuition proved right. Under his influence, Eve agreed to bite into the forbidden fruit, she even succeeded in turning her husband into an accomplice. (The moral of the story? Perhaps that everybody can be seduced: woman by Satan and man by woman.)

Here again, something in this episode will almost certainly disturb the careful reader. Is it conceivable that Eve could have hesitated even one second between the voice of the Creator of the Universe and that of the serpent, albeit a serpent on an extraordinary mission? We would find it easier to accept such a reaction from Adam; between the demand of heaven and the promises of woman, man may

18

well hesitate or else not hesitate at all. But Eve, how could she possibly disregard God's will and submit to the will of a serpent?

Here is what happened, according to legend. Obviously, it was all Eve's fault: she talked too much. Even before she tasted the forbidden fruit, she was guilty of exaggerating the facts. And as we all know, exaggeration leads to digression, which in turn leads straight to transgression.

Let us reread the text in the Book of Genesis: God instructs Adam and Eve not to *eat* of a certain fruit. Yet in her conversation with the serpent, Eve added something of her own to the prohibition: We were told not to eat from the tree and not even to *touch* it, for to do either would bring death upon us.

Lesson number one: fiction is dangerous business. Lesson number two: one must choose one's conversation partners with care and not talk to just anyone and surely not about theology. Eve's mistake was to enter into a dialogue with the serpent in the first place. Lesson number three: she was wrong in committing not only herself but her absent husband as well. Lesson number four: Adam should not have left his house; had he stayed home with his wife, the serpent would have had no chance of success. Eve had been an easy prey. The serpent knew just how to manipulate her. He knew that sin was one subject sure to interest Eve.

No sooner had Eve made the serpent's acquaintance than she was already telling him the story of the forbidden fruit; she could not refrain from disclosing that which,

1 9

after all, concerned only herself and her husband. And you really believe this? asked the serpent, looking surprised. You who are so intelligent, so perceptive, you actually believe that it is enough to touch the tree to die? When she did not answer, he walked up to the tree—and legend tells us the tree shouted with anger—and put his arms around it. You see, he said nonchalantly, I touched it and I am alive. Wouldn't you like to try it? Go ahead, you may, nothing will happen to you . . . Eve remained apprehensive and did not move. She was curious but distrustful. And then the serpent shoved her toward the tree. Eve saw the Angel of Death but stayed alive. Yet it was, for her and for us, the beginning of the end. The first contact with death. Caught in the treadmill, she ventured farther and farther. Too late to turn back, too late to erase what she had seen and experienced.

What Eve did not understand was that she would find in the forbidden fruit not death but the idea and the sensation of death; that it was possible for her to see the angel and not succumb.

She suddenly realized that life and death are not two separate domains; they meet in man, not in God. It is possible to live *with* death; all one needs to do is turn one's back on the living. It is possible to be dead and not know it.

But then, why did Eve commit the irreparable? What drove her to the serpent and why was it so important for her to touch the tree? Why didn't she stop in time? Could she have been—already then—attracted and fascinated by death, by nothingness?

The Midrash advances the following hypothesis: Eve was tempted by the promise of power. If you taste from the tree, the serpent had told her, you shall be like God, who ate from the same tree before creating the world; like Him, you shall have the power to create and destroy, to kill and resurrect. He convinced Eve that that was precisely what God had sought to prevent with his prohibition. She opted for the serpent's clever arguments over God's dry commandment. Clearly, she was ripe for seduction, though one may theorize that she considered the serpent an instrument rather than an accomplice and that she collaborated with him in order to establish her power.

Nor was the serpent fooled. His game simply became more sophisticated. Once he obtained a first concession from the woman; namely, that it was possible to touch the tree with impunity, he knew she would want to continue, to push ahead and test God by testing herself. Only now the serpent was saying no, invoking all sorts of pretexts. The more she wanted to bite into the fruit, the more he discouraged her. She pleaded with him, appealed to his feelings, reminded him of their friendship. Her excitement became unbearable. She had to eat this fruit no matter what the cost. Nothing else mattered any more; neither her dignity, her woman's pride, her fear, her security, nor her loyalty to her God, who was present, or to her husband, who was not. Driven by a passion she could no longer control, she knowingly courted disaster. She could not help herself; her curiosity and her greed were stronger than she.

Finally, the serpent agreed, but on one condition: that she share the fruit with her husband. And Eve—a woman to the end—could not resist the urge . . . to make another promise.

Then and only then did the serpent relent. He offered her the desired fruit. In passing, let me say that it was not an apple but a citrus. There are also those who say it was a bunch of grapes, while others maintain it was a fig. In any case, Eve took the fruit and held it in her hand, admiring its beauty, reluctant to swallow too quickly that which had cost her so dear. First she bit into the skin, careful not to eat the inside. Then she nibbled on a small piece—the effect was instantaneous: she discovered that she was mortal. For the first time she genuinely, deeply understood that there was a direct, inescapable relationship between her person and death. The game was up: God would keep His promise and strike. Instinctively she knew: He keeps His pledges, especially when it comes to punishment.

And yet, instead of desisting and repenting, she chose to use the serpent's stratagems on her husband and draw him into the same deadly trap. She already knew the price of disobeying God and yet she tricked Adam into becoming her accomplice. Since she would have to pay, she owed it to herself to drag Adam along. The Midrash stresses that Eve behaved like a jealous woman; the idea that her husband might survive—and possibly marry another— seemed intolerable to her. Since she had to die, she would not die alone.

But . . . where was Adam all that time? What was he doing while his wife arranged and rearranged his universe and changed his destiny? One text says he was asleep. Another, more charitable, assures us he was walking with God, who was showing him the world and teaching him to tame nature. The fact was that while Eve and the serpent were acting out their scene, Adam was elsewhere. Perhaps this was not unusual, perhaps his wife's constant chatter had finally irritated him. He must have yearned for a measure of peace and silence.

We said it earlier: Adam was a weakling. He remained passive while the world simmered around him. Unlike most mythological figures, he does not strike the reader as a leader of man, a giant who dictates his law. He demanded nothing, sought no glory. He built no empires, nor did he erect any temples. His modesty was such that he accepted to play a secondary role in his own tragedy.

Significantly, the tale of that tragedy is told by Eve— not Adam—in the apocryphal book named after them: *Sefer Adam ve Hava.* The tale, told in the first person, is as poignant as it is convincing. Toward the end of her life Eve gathered her children and her children's children around her: When I was young I met Satan in paradise. His face was shining and he sang the praises of the Almighty; I thought he was an angel, he seemed so pure. Then he seduced me into committing the one act I should not have committed . . .

In other words, she claimed to have fallen into Satan's trap because she could not have known that someone who looked like a friend could in fact be the enemy of mankind, bent on its corruption and eventual destruction. It wasn't my fault, not entirely, she seems to have told her grandchildren, I couldn't have known that certain faces wear masks . . . And indeed, how could she have guessed that Satan was Satan and not a messenger of God?

A frightening tale. How can one ever be sure of the authenticity of any prophet claiming to transmit the divine word? How can one ever be certain that the friend is not an impostor? All human dialogue is ambiguous. If Good always had the appearance of good and Evil could always be recognized, life would be simpler indeed. But it isn't simple. Not even in paradise.

How could Adam have suspected his wife of wishing his death? He believed in her and so had no thought of resisting, of stalling. Eve handed him the fruit and he bit into it. Immediately, without a question. He probably did not realize where the fruit had come from. Unlike Eve, Adam did not have the feeling of violating the supreme commandment. In his hand, in his mouth, the fruit was like any other. Only later did he understand his error: suddenly he was aware of his body, his nakedness, his own vulnerability. He felt lost, his home was broken, life was against him. How could he ever trust anyone again? His own wife had deceived him, perhaps even doomed him. Once he had bitten into the forbidden fruit, Adam turned into a tragic figure.

And man's history could begin—at last.

The rest we know. The Bible tells us that the couple was chased from paradise. The Midrash, with lavish use of imagery, goes on to describe the events and their consequences in great detail. At first, these were merely physical: Adam's body grew smaller and smaller. Then they became spiritual as well: he lost his powers over the animals. He no longer radiated light. Worse, for the first time he discovered the meaning of anguish and fear. Whereas before he had stood proudly erect as he listened to God, he now tried to escape His voice. Where are you? God asked him. And the celebrated Rebbe Shneur-Zalmen of Ladi comments: What? God didn't know where Adam was hiding? No. This is a question God asks of every man, always: Where are you? What is your place in the world? What are you doing with your life . . . ? Still, the Midrash believes that Adam, shamed by his sin, was actually trying to hide. And God had to admonish him: Tell me, man, you who are hiding—do you really believe the house can hide from its builder?

Adam was no longer the same. He saw death everywhere. Objects, images, feelings, words, impulses—everything revolved around his obsession with death. The sun went down? A sign that my end is near, I shall lose consciousness in the dark. The sun is rising? Surely it will burn me. A stranger to the world and to himself, he no longer knew where to look, what signs to watch for. Who were his enemies, where were they lying in wait for him? Everywhere and within himself. He was afraid to make a move, to utter a word. Unknown forces beset and chained him down. He was convinced that it was written all over him: the beasts and animals he once had tamed now looked at him in a different way. With hate. As soon as they saw him, they fell silent. And when he listened to his own heart, he found it empty of joy and desire. Fear, black and biting fear, was his only companion. Expelled from paradise, he entered time.

In the hut they had built for themselves, the man and the woman began to repent; for seven days and seven nights they mourned the death of their innocence. Then, unable to bear it any longer, Eve—romantic even in misfortune—turned to her husband with a suggestion that is to her credit: Since I am the one responsible for our shared suffering, since I am the one who made you go astray, kill me and surely God will let you reenter paradise. Adam refused, of course; he knew that no one can undo what has been done; that no one can change the past. And also that it is not by giving death to another that death can be defeated.

The Midrash thus shows us Eve in a new light: lucid and penitent. She knew now that her husband was innocent and she was not; she acknowledged that it would be unjust to make Adam share her punishment.

In fact, one text goes even further and suggests that she herself was a victim of injustice, and not guilty, not really, not entirely. After all, the first couple *had* to violate the divine commandment to allow mankind to evolve. Had Adam and Eve opted for life and against knowledge, history would have ended with them. There would have been no punishment, no death, no struggle for survival, no nothing, no nobody. Adam and Eve *had* to defy God so that their descendants might sing His praises. They were not free, hence not responsible.

But then, why the punishment? The Midrash says they were punished not so much for having sinned as for having invented excuses and alibis. Adam placed the blame on Eve, and Eve placed it on the serpent. Their greatest sin was to have shunned their responsibilities.

Another explanation suggests that injustice is inherent in man's fate. God is omniscient, yet every man is responsible for his own freedom. Man is trapped; even when he opposes God, he is but accomplishing His will—which does not mitigate his punishment.

Could that be the reason why Adam and Eve sinned with such lack of constraint? To rebel against this iniquity? As if to say: You could have prevented us from sinning; You did not. So be it, only now we shall do so freely, consciously, even deliberately. This may have been their chance to cry out against the incomprehensible laws of Him who wishes to be the Father and Judge of man.

They were not the first to rebel; we know there were precedents. When God decided to create man, the earth simply refused to yield her clay. The moon objected to having to share its duties and privileges with the sun. Even the waters rejected the divine decree dividing them into upper and lower waters. Yet man alone was punished severely. Why? Perhaps because his rebellion alone had been conceived and willed by God.

Adam's fall, just or not, constitutes the most dramatic chapter of his long life. Outside paradise, he became real. Rejected by God, he drew closer to Eve. Never were the two so united. Suddenly they discovered a purpose to their existence: to perfect the world which until then had been no more than created. To use the experience that had been theirs. To transmit. To communicate by deed and word. To safeguard. To tell the tale, omitting nothing, forgetting nothing. To keep alive the memory of his past, Adam had taken four plants from paradise as proof that his tales, his obsessions were more than dreams. True, he suffered whenever he looked at them; true, the old grief was now deeper and all-pervasive, but never mind, the challenge lay in defeating oblivion, not pain. He could have thrown away the plants, instead he guarded them jealously. To forget would have solved nothing.

Not content to live with the vestiges of the past, Adam and Eve planned their future. They built a house on the ruins of their shattered existence. Alone. Without outside help. They worked on fashioning their future, their own immortality. Eve bore Adam two sons, Cain and Abel. In the apocryphal "The Testament of Henoch" we find the following tale. One morning Eve tells her husband: I had a nightmare; I saw Cain kill his brother . . . The first nightmare in history. And like the others, it later came true.

The years went by. The couple had a third son, Seth. They loved him; he was their hope. One Midrash has it that Adam gave him a book and that this book was the Torah. He thus placed on Seth the responsibility of transmitting its teachings to his sons and their sons after them, to the end of all generations.

Then Adam, who was old and weak, fell sick. His grandchildren gathered around his sickbed: What is the matter with you, Grandfather? — I am sick. — What exactly does that mean, to be sick? — I feel pain. — Pain, what is that . . . ? The gap between the generations had become wide enough to be apparent; each one had its own preoccupations. Adam spoke and his grandchildren did not understand. He suffered and his grandchildren could not know.

Only Eve and Seth shared in his sorrow. They went and knocked on the gate to paradise, seeking assistance, pleading for an herb potent enough to cure all ailments. But they were turned away and their request refused. They insisted, they wept. In vain. Finally, they were told the truth: Adam was to live no longer; his time had come to die.

Adam thus bequeathed us his death—his death and not

his sin. The concept of original sin is alien to Jewish tradition. We do not inherit the sins of our fathers, even though we may be made to endure their punishment. Guilt cannot be transmitted. We are linked to Adam only by his memory, which becomes our own, and by his death, which foreshadows our own. Not by his sin.

Midrashic literature contains magnificent and detailed descriptions of his funeral. Processions of angels and seraphim escorted him straight to paradise, where he still dwells. From there he watches his descendants leaving one world for the other. And as they tear themselves away from the living, they in turn are watching him. No man dies, says the Zohar, without seeing Adam and questioning him about his guilt. On his deathbed every man turns to Adam with the reproach: It is because of *your* sin that I must die.

Legend claims that this was precisely what Adam feared most. Therefore he pleaded with God never to reveal the true nature of his guilt. One text claims that his wish was granted; that the full story of what took place under the Tree would never be told. But then, of course, another source states the opposite. No matter; Adam found a way to defend himself. Whenever a mortal reminds him of his transgression, he replies: I have committed only one sin—you have committed many; every man is responsible for his own death.

But Adam must *see* men, his progeny, die. *That* is his punishment; it is as though he were dying over and over again. He dies *with* and *in* every dying man, and together with every mortal he awaits the coming of the Messiah, who will abolish death. Adam's fate is no longer his own; it belongs to anyone who claims it as his own.

Adam's real punishment? Once he had been at peace with the world. No more. Once he had been monolithic, whole. No more. After the fall he was a broken man. One part of him remained in paradise while the other continued to dream of it with nostalgia. One part of him yearned for God, the other for escape from God. Paraphrasing the Talmudic injunction, one could say: No man may study the secrets of creation except to restore his oneness to the man who incarnates the beginning of man.

What does Adam represent for us, today? True, his destiny is unique, but that is true for every one of us. Every man must believe that his every deed involves all other men. Whoever kills, kills Adam. Whoever kills, kills Adam's vision, kills in Adam's name. Every man should be Adam to all others. That is the lesson learned—or to be learned—from his adventure.

Nor is it the only one. Expelled from paradise, Adam and Eve did not give in to resignation. In the face of death they decided to fight by giving life, by conferring a meaning on life. After the fall they began to work, to strive for a future marked by man. Their children would die—never mind! One moment of life contains eternity, one moment of life is worth eternity.

Here again Adam differs from most other mythological figures. Though defeated by God, he did not wallow in self-denial. He had the courage to get up and begin anew. He understood that though man is doomed from the start, he can and must act freely when planning his future. Such is the essence of Jewish tradition. Despite his fall, Adam died undaunted. As long as he lived, even far from paradise, even far from God, victory belonged not to death but to him.

According to Jewish tradition, creation did not end with man, it began with him. When He created man, God gave him a secret—and that secret was not how to begin but how to begin again.

In other words, it is not given to man to begin; that privilege is God's alone. But it is given to man to begin again—and he does so every time he chooses to defy death and side with the living. Thus he justifies the ancient plan of the most ancient of men, Adam, to whom we are bound both by the anguish that oppressed him and the defiance that elevated him above the paradise we shall never enter.

PARABLES AND
SAYINGS I

A Midrashic saying: Man who is mortal and limited
cannot grasp the secrets of creation; they exist and he knows
it. That must suffice. This is why it is written in the Book
of Books that in the beginning God created the heavens and
the earth, without saying how.

A story: A pagan paid a visit to Rabbi Akiba in order to
taunt him.
— Who created the world? he asked.
— God, blessed-be-His-name, replied the sage.
— Really? Then prove it.
— Very well, said Rabbi Akiba. Come back tomorrow.
The pagan returned the following day.
— What are you wearing? asked the sage.
— That's a strange question, said the pagan. I am wear-
ing a suit.
— Really? And who made it?
— The tailor.

33

— Prove it, said Rabbi Akiba.

Whereupon the pagan became angry.

— What, don't you know that it is the tailor who made the clothes we wear?

To which the sage replied:

— And you don't know that it is God who made this world we live in?

The pagan went away.

Having witnessed the two exchanges, Rabbi Akiba's disciples expressed surprise: they could see no connection. And so the sage explained:

— Know this, children, that just as the house attests to the builder and the garment to the tailor and the door to the carpenter, the world is and will be God's testimonial; one has only to look at it to understand that what it affirms is God.

Said Rabbi Shimon: On this earth everything is arranged in accordance with a divine plan. The blade of grass grows only because, up above, an angel incites it to do so, saying: Grow, for such is the will of God.

A parable: On the third day, having given sap and seed to the plants and the trees, God encountered unexpected problems. The tall cedars of Lebanon seemed too tall, almost arrogant. And so God decided to create iron. The trees understood the threat and began to weep: Woe unto us, for we shall all be felled by the ax. But God reassured them:

34

Without handle, the ax is but a hunk of iron. Since the handle is made of wood, try to live in peace without betraying one another, stay united and the iron will be powerless against you.

A saying: The following preceded the creation of the world—the Torah, the celestial throne, the patriarchs, Israel, the Temple and the name of the Messiah.

Commented Rabbi Akiba on the verse And God saw all that He had made and found it very good: *King David was right to admire the miraculous variety of the Almighty's works: there exist creatures who live only in the water and others who subsist only on land; let the former venture outside the water and they will perish; let the latter enter the water and they will drown. Then there are creatures who live in the fire and others who thrive in the air; let the former breathe air and they will die; let the latter come near the fire and they will burn. Oh yes, in God's scheme, every species has its own domain, its very own world.*

A saying from the Zohar: On the sixth day, having created man, God said to him: I have worked heretofore, now you shall continue.

A Hasidic story: A disciple made the following remark in front of Rebbe Menahem-Mendl of Kotzk: God, who is

3 5

perfect, took six days to create a world that is not, how is that possible? The rebbe scolded him:

— *Could you have done better?*

— *Yes, I think so, stammered the disciple, who no longer knew what he was saying.*

— *You could have done better? the Master cried out. Then what are you waiting for? You don't have a minute to waste, go ahead, start working!*

Says the Midrash: The world we know is not the only one that God has created. God is forever building new ones and then destroying them, for they give Him no pleasure.

CAIN AND ABEL:
THE FIRST
GENOCIDE

O<small>N THE SURFACE</small>, the tale of Cain and Abel, this tale of absolute crime and absolute punishment, is reminiscent of today's theater of the absurd. Between crime and punishment there appears to be no connection save that of the narratives, which are identical: killer and victim share the same story.

And a gloomy story it is: drab and devoid of beauty, tragic or otherwise, and truth, divine or otherwise—even though it describes a threefold confrontation: between man and God, at once present and hidden, between man and his brother, at once rivals and associates, and ultimately between man and himself, oscillating between good and evil, malediction and grace—timeless forces acting one against the other, one inside the other.

It is the curious and frightening tale of two brothers who, jealous of each other's belongings, memories and solitude, are unable to coexist in a world they are still alone to possess. And so they call on death to be their arbiter, thus forever justifying darkness and doom—their own and ours.

What we have here is not yet the defiance of a father, Abraham, who much later challenged the Father of all men by leading his son to the altar at His command. Nor are we any longer dealing with the dream that the first man, Adam, in his first dazzling awakening, formed of his destiny and ours.

The place is everywhere, anywhere. The time is after the beginning, after creation, after Shabbat. Hence, the odd feeling of letdown, perhaps guilt, a feeling which normally follows creation, any creation—this is true for any artist, even the Greatest of all. Gloom hangs over the universe; the celebration is over, heaven has left earth behind. God's creatures are tired. Disillusioned, disenchanted.

We may assume that Adam still felt the effects of the initial creative thrust of cosmic discovery, of the first surprise, that of the disciple admiring the Master's work. This is no longer true of his sons; they remember only the fall.

There followed a period of transition when man was no longer alone but not yet mortal, therefore not yet fully conscious of his powers and shortcomings. His past was limited to his physical memory, he still did not have a future, yet he was no longer free to reject it: he was condemned to live. Irresistibly drawn to the unknown—though afraid of it—he moved forward, steadily, inexorably, toward murder and remorse. Irrevocable, his act was carried out in bloodshed and not in fervor. Irreversible, his search ended in senseless brutality, in darkness and not in prayer.

It is a disquieting story, one that contains no call, no transcending quest; nor does it open gates of hidden sanctuaries. It suggests evil on its lowest, most primitive level. Raw, unembellished instincts dictate the rules of the game; instincts and not divine command. Here, God tested neither the killer nor the victim; their acts were committed freely, stupidly. Without understanding, without even trying to understand.

And yet these two individuals had everything to stir our emotions; both were marked, doomed. Cain: the first assassin and perhaps the first man to view murder as an act of ultimate rebellion. Abel: the first victim, the first man to leave this world in silence, without a word of regret, without a gesture of protest.

Why did Cain choose violence and his brother resignation? Why did neither resist the role assigned to him: Cain that of executioner and Abel that of victim?

We do not understand them, yet in an obscure way we feel involved in their fate. Their adventure is that of the first genocide, foreshadowing more than one war. Their behavior is familiar to us; every one of their impulses prefigures our conduct in stress situations. Ultimately we are confronted by them, or rather by their image, the image of a man with two faces we cannot contemplate without fear. Yes, fear is the name of their tale, bottomless, hopeless fear, unconquerable and precluding any possibility of redemption. Cain and Abel: *they* were mankind.

39

The choice was limited and absolute: assassin or victim, nothing else. Assassin or victim: without onlooker or witness. God? God is judge. God is participant. Accomplice.

But why is this lugubrious episode told to us? What is it meant to reveal, to prove, to affirm, to refute. No narration is more debasing, no event more destructive. Why should it be remembered today and always? Why should we be compelled to look at these two enemy brothers whenever our gaze probes the horizon or reverts to our beginnings?

No other Biblical situation contains so many questions or arouses so many uncertainties.

Let us examine the text. The event is presented in a few terse sentences heavy with allusions, with a density rare even in the Bible. The style is sober, spare; the pace is quick and harrowing. Only the essentials are given: names, vocations, conflicts: loveless lives, hateless killings. A few misunderstood impulses, a few wrongly interpreted silences, and the drama is set: the loving comradeship between brothers, the friendship between adolescents degenerate into disaster.

We could read this taut linear narrative as a tragedy in three acts with a cast of three to be played three times and on three different levels. At the first reading, Cain would be the villain. At the second, it would be Abel. At the third, it would be He who manipulated them.

• • •

Let us listen.

Once upon a time there lived a man named Cain who had a brother named Abel. Called upon to share their parents' haunted kingdom, they quarreled over heavenly favors and finally confronted one another in every role that defines man's relationship to other men.

Though born on the same day, according to the Midrash, Cain was the older of the two. When he was born, his mother boasted: *Kaniti ish et adoshem,* which literally means: I bought a man with God. Figuratively, it could mean something else: for the first time there was human collaboration in the creation of a man; for the first time a human being was entirely human, that is to say, man's work and also man's responsibility. Cain was the exclusive concern of his parents; God was not involved. This may explain his temperament: demanding, arrogant, distrustful, prone to abrupt changes in mood. He was a doer who considered himself free to do whatever he chose. A strange, misunderstood man, yearning for conquests and honors, he had to affirm himself, he had to win; otherwise he was unhappy, resentful, hating the whole world, himself most of all.

Abel, his poor younger brother, was more appealing. He is pictured as a romantic shepherd, gentle and timid, a dreamer of kind and peaceful dreams. A tireless pilgrim, a lover of roads and wind who felt at home nowhere;

indeed, had no home, nor wanted one. He roamed through the world in wonder, marveling at the rustling of leaves or simply at being alive, at being capable of giving and receiving. The very epitome of the man-child.

One day the two brothers, for different reasons no doubt, brought offerings to God. And God, for reasons unknown, accepted those of Abel but rejected those of Cain. Cain flew into a rage, and instead of quarreling with God, turned against his brother and slew him.

In the next scene we find God in the role of prosecutor. He did not accuse Cain of murder, not yet. Good investigator that He is, He used kindness to snare His suspect, asking an innocent question in a rather friendly tone: Would you, by any chance, know where your brother might be? As though He did not know. Or as though He did not want Cain to know that He knew. And Cain, who had not yet understood that God is God and that He is silence and secret, fell into the trap and answered: My brother? No idea; am I supposed to be his keeper? Only then did God lay his cards on the table: *Kol dmei akhiha tzoakim elai min haadama*—I hear thy brother's voice howling from the depths of the earth. The French call this *coup de théâtre,* the dramatic, unexpected moment that changes the direction and tone of a play and the axis around which it revolves. Suddenly Cain's arrogance was gone; he was caught and he knew it. He became very humble and accepted his fate with contrition: *My sin is too great, too great to be borne . . . Shall I hide before Thy face . . . ?*

4 2

The epilogue? Cursed but alive, Cain turned into a wanderer like his slain brother before him and, like his brother, he was murdered by a blood relative. Having removed Abel, Cain became Abel and inherited his fate though not his innocence.

There are gaps in the text. From the purely human point of view, we cannot but be disturbed about . . . the parents.

After all, Adam and Eve were still alive and even quite well, considering the circumstances. What were *they* doing while their children were quarreling? Could they not have intervened? Used their parental authority? Remonstrated with the one and appeased the other? Could they not have reasoned with them, explained to them, calmly but firmly, what life, and particularly collective life, was all about? Granted that Cain was a problem child, why then did Adam—or Eve—not try to intercede on his behalf, attempt to improve his relations with God?

Well, actually, Adam could not be found. He had disappeared. Vanished. At the very moment when his presence was most needed. While Cain was in trouble with God and Abel was pitted against Cain, Adam was conspicuously absent. As though the education and problems of his sons were no concern of his. He was the busy father, overworked and self-involved, earning his bread by the sweat of his brow. Well, maybe. But then, where was Eve? Did she but try, just once, to act as buffer between Cain and

God, between Cain and his brother? Where was *she* when her turbulent and precocious children needed a mother to arbitrate between them, to scold and love them? How are we to explain this first and probably most fatal pedagogical failure in history? Must we attribute it to the "gap" that separates all generations, those of long ago and today's, and the resulting lack of communication and understanding between parents and their children?

No less serious are the theological questions. Why did God choose to commit the first act of discrimination between men? Why indeed did he favor Abel over his brother? Because, as we are told by the Midrash, his offerings were superior? Did the gifts' value really matter to God? To God too? Or did He prefer Abel because he had the advantage of being weak—God loves the weak—and young, for even God likes to please the young?

Or was there another reason? Cain was in constant motion, troubling, disturbing, speaking incessantly, whereas his brother liked to meditate and listen. Was that a reason for God to side with one against the other? Or did God wish to make the point—even then—that injustice is inherent in the human condition; that two human beings—no matter who they are or who their grandparents were—are never equal, since their duties and privileges are never the same? That therefore men could be brothers and still could not claim equal rights? How is one to understand God's arbitrary way of handling His creatures, playing one man against the other, turning them into irreconcilable enemies?

Cain, after all, was guilty of no wrongdoing; he had transgressed no interdiction. Not yet. Indeed, he had not done or said *anything* as yet. Even his thoughts about God seem almost irreproachable. Like his brother, and much before him, he tried to please Him, to pay Him homage. The offerings were his idea. Abel but imitated him. And what did Cain receive in exchange? A rejection. Why? Why this gratuitous, public humiliation? Worse: when God finally did speak to him, He scored him for being disappointed, using cruel, obscure language: Why are you so resentful and why has your countenance fallen? Surely, if you do right, it shall mean exaltation. But if you do wrong, sin is the demon at the door, urging you to follow. Still, you can be his master . . . Cain, in the absence of any explanation, expected at least some consolation; instead he was treated to a lecture on morality and a warning. Offended, unjustly rejected, encumbered with offerings nobody wanted, what was he to do? Hush his grief, contain his sorrow? Nobody ever taught him how. It was only normal for him to unburden himself, to justify retroactively the injustice perpetrated on him, by giving in to the violence rumbling inside him, by striking out and killing.

That is the impression emanating from the text. Repudiated by God, Cain sank into a black depression. Whereupon God, with a cruelty as startling as it was unprovoked, asked why he looked so crestfallen, why he was so depressed. As though He did not know, as though He was not the cause!

Judging by the tone and rhythm of the verbal exchange, it would appear that God was doing His utmost to multiply the pressures on Cain and push him to the limits of his endurance. By rejecting him, by ridiculing him, by denying his acts all spiritual meaning, God seems to have tried to create a kind of maladjustment: Cain would no longer know the difference between what was just and what was not. He witnessed the sudden collapse of his universe. He no longer knew what to do with a life that now seemed shallow and useless. How could he fill its void and give it meaning? He set out to find a deed that would not be lost, but would be inscribed in time, in a memory other than his own. He was the outsider, who kills to feel alive, to penetrate reality, to accelerate the cause of events, to arrive more quickly at the inevitable and inevitably tragic end. Conditioned for this kind of spectacular, definitive gesture, Cain could not help but kill: he did not choose the crime; instead, the crime chose him.

Here we face a totally different question: If Cain was truly conditioned to commit murder, why do we not look upon him as a victim of God, just as we consider Abel a victim of man?

Abel is an obvious victim; indeed, he is victim personified. That was his function from the beginning; his very name signifies futility, vanity. Every victim throughout the ages was and is meant to recognize himself in him. Like him, these victims seem to exist for the sole purpose of enduring, suffering and eventually disappearing. They exist to allow the murderer to satisfy his craving for bloodshed. And that is precisely what troubles us in Abel's story. We cannot understand why, and by what right, God gave him life. Why did he bring him into the world? To be used by the murderer? What sin had he committed to deserve such punishment? A Midrash tells us: *Ein mita belo khet*—There is no death without sin. And what about Abel? A sinner, a criminal, he? No, he was but a poor dreamer, innocent and pure. One of the Just Men, he is counted among the fathers of mankind. One legend claims that he lived only fifty days—surely somewhat too short a time to have transgressed the most important commandments of the Torah.

Inevitably we must ask: Assuming that God did need a villain, why did He want Abel to be His victim? What criteria did He apply when casting the roles? Why did Abel deserve to die so young, without having had a chance to make something of his life?

Sensitive to the complexities and inner tensions of the Biblical narrative, the Midrash, as usual, tries to adorn it with details and commentaries, the Midrash being to the Bible what imagination is to knowledge. But in this particular instance, the commentators seem intimidated by the subject. Rabbi Shimon Bar-Yohai has left us this sentence: *Kashe hadavar lemro veii efshar lape lefarsho*—This episode cannot be expressed in words, nor is it possible to comment on its implications.

In fact, there is less Midrashic material about Cain and

47

Abel than about any other Biblical figure. We are told much about Abraham and his father, Moses and his brother, Pharaoh and his counselors. Using Midrashic texts, we can reconstruct their portraits. But not those of Cain and Abel. The only attempt to leave us a description, however sketchy, of Cain was made by his grandson, Lemekh . . . who was blind. The rabbinical chroniclers evidently concluded that the event led too far, further than the one that later took place on Mount Moriah; for Isaac was saved, Abel was not.

And yet the Talmud does, however reluctantly, offer a variety of explanations for this first murder in history, covering it from every possible angle. Our sages exerted themselves trying to explain the tragedy; some based their thesis on materialistic motives, others on sexual impulses, still others on religious considerations, so that every passion that ever fanned a war would be named and every taste satisfied.

First hypothesis: Cain and Abel quarreled over strictly material possessions, two brothers at odds over their parents' heritage—but what a heritage: the whole world. Cain appropriated all the real estate while Abel took everything else. The conflict broke out when the older of the two, greedy and dissatisfied, wanted to expel his brother from his domain: The ground on which you are walking is mine, leave it; you may fly if you wish. The air does not belong to me, but the ground is mine. The little brother's retort was quick in coming: Perfect. But in that case take off the clothes you're wearing; the wool they are made of comes from my flock and the flock is mine, therefore so is the wool. One word led to another, one insult to another, the quarrel turned violent. And God suddenly realized that words can lead to murder.

This explanation, appealing as it may be to those who would consider economic tensions as the cause of most evils, is tenuous at best. It does not take into consideration the fact that the two brothers could not in any way share in their parents' heritage for the simple reason that both their parents were still alive. True, Adam and Eve were getting on in years, yet they were not as old as all that, since they eventually had a third son, Seth. What right did Cain and Abel have to claim properties that were not theirs? Were they trying to take them over unlawfully? And why did their parents not object?

Confronted with this difficulty, the Talmud advances a second theory: *cherchez la femme.* Yes, a woman must be responsible, the question is which one? Again, there are two theories.

1. The brothers quarreled over the woman in their life: Adam's second wife and their mother, Eve. (And whatever Freud will have to say about Oedipus and the complex that bears his name will be nothing but commentary.)

2. The woman was none other than Abel's twin sister, whom one source describes as having been the world's most beautiful woman. Cain was determined to marry her. So was his young brother, which complicated matters.

49

Cain invoked the right of seniority, Abel that of simultaneity: we were brought into the world together, said he, together we shall remain.

Thus, whether mother or sister, woman would be responsible for the first fratricidal war in history; because of a lover's disappointment, Cain lost his soul, Abel his life and we, their fellow-men, our good conscience.

This theory will surely appeal to some. The trouble is that no reference to a sister can be found in Scripture. Surely the Bible could have managed to give her a name, an identity; it could even have asked her whether she had a preference between the two pretenders.

Was it their mother they coveted, after all? Here again the explanation is not satisfactory. Would Adam not have had something to say in the matter?

And so we come to the third and last possibility: that the conflict revolved around religion or at least matters of some spiritual concern. Since Cain and Abel had to share the universe, the older had chosen the here-and-now and his brother the world-to-come. However, Cain soon demanded more; namely, a share in the other world as well. When Abel refused to relinquish any part of it, Cain flew into a rage and killed him.

An image: the two brothers fought over the Temple in Jerusalem. Each wanted it for his own. The family quarrel would thus actually have been a religious war. A mystical motive, which paradoxically seems the most rational: Jerusalem has indeed continued to cause bloodshed throughout the centuries.

Unfortunately, here again manifold and varied objections and contradictions appear. In principle, the world-to-come was promised to all men and no one could exclude anyone else. Only God could decide whether to let Cain enter or not. Only God could open or close the celestial gates. And so Abel is thought to have overstepped his limits. As for the Temple, how could Abel even contemplate erecting it on his land, since, legally, he had none to call his own?

This last theory thus would place the blame on Abel, whose behavior was both unreasonable and unwarranted, rather than on Cain. Cain had every right to become annoyed. Abel really did go too far: he was taking advantage of his brother. He who owned not a parcel of land in the whole world, tried to claim the most precious of all to build the holiest edifice of all. Cain would not have been human had he not reacted with rage.

Clearly, these explanations must not be taken literally. Cain and Abel are symbols, examples meant to illustrate the main motivations that drive individuals to hate, bloodshed, war and, ultimately, self-destruction: sexual obsession, material power and religious fanaticism—or just plain fanaticism.

Yet the event remains unexplained; the file remains open. However logical or ingenious, none of the theses presented is irrefutable. We grope in the dark. We still do not know why Cain killed and why Abel did not resist.

While conducting its investigation, should the Midrash not have asked the elementary, the key question asked by any detective: Who benefited from the crime? Well, it did not ask, and for good reason: the question is troublesome, for it implicates someone other than the assassin. In any case, there is no need to look for the assassin; his identity is known from the start. What escapes us is the motive. In other circumstances, the Midrash might have had recourse to the convenient and devoted services of Satan and saddled him with the responsibility. Not this time. The Midrash was well aware that all questions and all answers must begin and end with man: even those questions to which there is no answer.

(Where are questions allowed to remain unanswered? In art, particularly in literature. And that is how the Talmud views Cain and Abel—as characters in a novel. And why not? We know that a bad novel has three characters: the famous triangle. A good novel has only two. A great novel limits itself to one. Did Cain eliminate Abel for purely literary reasons?)

As for the murder itself, the Midrash does nothing to elude it or to mitigate its horror. On the contrary, it furnishes us with a rather realistic, almost visual description. The two enemy brothers were alone, with no one to incite or appease them. They were not playing; they did what they meant to do. They were determined to examine everything, to get to the bottom of things. A settling of accounts that had to end badly. When Abel panicked and ran, Cain stormed after him in pursuit. Abel climbed a hill with Cain at his heels. And so they bounded from mountaintop to valley, from valley to forest, from one end of the world to the other, from one world to the other; until finally there they stood, face to face, breathless and fierce, until they locked in a final struggle, the fatal embrace. And then, abruptly, the Midrash shifts, and we see the characters in a different light. Till then we were shown a powerful, almost invincible Cain, who forced his foe into flight. Suddenly, without any transition, Abel emerges as the stronger of the two. The frail and awkward dreamer gained the upper hand. And when Cain, distraught and unrecognizable, begged for pardon and mercy, Abel pretended not to hear. But Cain knew his weak point—his parents: Abel, my brother, we are alone here; if you come home without me, what will you tell our parents? And Abel, imagining his mother and father in mourning, opened himself to pity. He loosened his grip. Cain saw his chance: swift as a wild beast, he jumped to his feet and struck. And killed. Abel had fallen victim to his own pity.

The next scene, more dramatic, makes even greater demands on our imagination: the accused confronts his judge.

Cain was too clever to deny the facts, too shrewd to confess; instead he resorted to humor. Less sullen, more talkative, he seems changed by the murder. He devised a system of defense that included the use of irony: Master of the Universe, it seems that I am accused of murder; who is my accuser? My parents who live here on earth know nothing. How did You get Your information? Is it possible that there are informers up there?

Later he tried to use reason: Master of the Universe, let us be logical. I have never seen a corpse, I don't know what death is; how could I know that it is enough to strike a man . . . to kill him?

He appears even more resourceful when, feigning indignation, he launched his counterattack: Master of the Universe, You declare me guilty? Guilty, me? Guilty of what? Of having been caught? Imagine a thief apprehended in a forbidden garden; he could tell the watchman: My job is to steal and yours is to prevent me from stealing; if I succeeded in entering the garden, whose fault is that? You are the watchman of the world. If You did not wish me to kill my brother, why did You not intervene?

Rabbi Shimon Bar-Yohai illustrates this idea with a parable: Two athletes fight to entertain the king. At the outcome of the contest will the victor be indicted for murder?

For Shimon Bar-Yohai, a fervent mystic, Cain and Abel were equals, endowed with the same privileges, the same virtues; neither was more just or had more merit than the other. Only later, in the third century, was Cain turned into a monster, the forerunner of killers. Earlier rabbinical literature depicts him as more human. Some sages assert that he had prophetic gifts, since he invoked the future for the needs of his defense: Six hundred thousand Jews will

54

commit sins in the desert, and You will forgive them. Why then would You not forgive me?

According to the Biblical text, Cain was condemned to exile in perpetuity, not to death. He even enjoyed a strange immunity; no one had the right to imitate him by killing him. Was he protected by God? Yes. But also by his deed. Having done something nobody before him had ever done, he became untouchable, isolated by the newness and enormity of his crime. He left the country and became a builder of cities. So as to live in one? Probably. But what of the divine judgment condemning him to wandering? Does it mean that one can remain in one place and still be in exile? Probably. Exile is not necessarily linked to geography.

Time went by. One day Cain met his aging father, who asked him how things were going. He told him everything. The murder. The trial. The remorse. The penance. The atonement. God wants man to be redeemable, always. And Adam was moved to compose a song, *Mizmor Shir leyom ha-Shabbat,* a song celebrating the seventh day; the first human song was one of gratitude.

And so the narrative, now serene, approaches its ending —and a happy ending it is: Cain, the personification of brutal crime, of lying cynicism, constitutes living proof that pardon is possible, thus justifying hope in man's renewal, if not in his fate.

• • •

55

Yet the enigma remains: Why did Cain kill? What drove him to murder? For once, the Biblical tale, for all its sobriety and terseness, gives us more clues than its Midrashic commentaries.

Let us go back to Abel. We examined the fact and the extent of his guilt or complicity. Even assuming that Cain *had* to kill, why did Abel deserve to be killed? Let us reread the text: God accepted Abel's offerings but not those of Cain, who became bitter and sank into a deep depression. God then aggravated his sorrow by pretending not to know, by speaking of the future while forgetting the past, in other words, by ignoring his grief. Locking himself into the silence of his despair, Cain did not answer. He was angry with God but not with his brother. Not yet. He forgave him for having stolen his idea, his gesture, for having outdone him by bringing better offerings than his own. When he finally felt the need to speak, to confide, he turned not to God—nor to his parents—but to his brother. Rejecting dialogue with God, *vayomer Cain el Hebel akhiv* —Cain spoke to his brother, Abel. What did he say? We don't know. Perhaps he simply repeated to him the words he had just heard. It hardly seems to matter. Cain, grief-stricken, wanted to, had to, unburden himself. All he wanted was someone to talk to, to commune with. To feel a presence. And break his solitude. To have a brother, an ally when confronting God.

And Abel? Abel remained aloof. He did nothing to console his brother, to cheer him up or appease him. He who was responsible for Cain's sorrow did nothing to help him. He regretted nothing, said nothing. He simply was not there, he was present without being present. No doubt he was dreaming of better worlds, of holy things. Cain spoke to him and he did not listen. Or else he listened but did not hear. Therein lay his guilt. In the face of suffering, one has no right to turn away, not to see. In the face of injustice, one may not look the other way. When someone suffers, and it is not you, he comes first. His very suffering gives him priority. When someone cries, and it is not you, he has rights over you even if his pain has been inflicted by your common God. To watch over a man who grieves is a more urgent duty than to think of God. Though too weak to oppose God, man is strong enough to defend his fellow-man or at least to dress his wounds. Abel did nothing—such was the nature of his fault.

So much for Abel. But what about Cain? If Abel was guilty, does that mean Cain was innocent? Not at all. Cain should have understood his brother's tragedy: to be chosen by God is no less painful and restrictive than to incur His wrath. Man punishes those who love him, God chastises those He loves. In either case the punishment is unjust: to live with God causes no less anguish than to live without Him or against Him. When he saw God's hand stretched toward Abel, singling him out, Cain should have felt sorry for him, for man pays dearly for God's favors. By envying Abel, by refusing to understand him, to love him *in spite* of everything, by judging him and thus repudiating him, Cain became guilty. He was guilty even *before* he killed; his murderous deed only brought to a climax that which was already there.

Why did he do it? Perhaps he wanted to remain alone: an only child and, after his parents' death, the only man. Alone like God and perhaps alone in place of God. Like God, he thought to offer himself a human sacrifice in holocaust. He wanted to be cruel like Him, a stranger like Him, an avenger like Him. And like Him, present and absent at the same time, absent by his presence, present *in* his absence. Cain killed to become God. To kill God.

Cain, then, in his desire to achieve a kind of transfiguration, tried to disfigure mankind by forcing absolute guilt upon it by his crime. He killed to kill. To destroy what existed. To assassinate man. Any man who takes himself for God ends up assassinating men.

But let us be fair and examine the inverse hypothesis: what if Cain killed *for* man, to demonstrate that man is capable of usurping the role of death and remain human?

This concept is unacceptable and outside Jewish tradition, in which the deed is what counts. A saint who kills is a killer. A preacher who tortures is a sadist. No man may play with another man's life. No man ever kills *for* man—or *for* God. Every murder is against man and against God. Son of the first man, Cain lost his privileges from the moment he had blood on his hands.

The word *brother* keeps returning in the text, on the surface a superfluous reminder; we know they are brothers. Yet the word is repeated over and over to stress a fundamental principle: whoever kills, kills his brother; and when one has killed, one no longer is anyone's brother. One is the enemy.

This brings us to the leitmotif of this tale: responsibility. The two brothers were responsible one for the other. Neither was entirely guilty or totally innocent; both were, each in his own way, indifferent to the other.

When God asked Cain: Where is Abel, your brother? Cain answered: *Lo yadati, hashomer akhi anokhi?*—I didn't know, am I my brother's keeper? In the spirit of the Midrash, I would suggest that a different punctuation of the verse, eliminating the comma, would change the meaning to: I didn't know I was supposed to be my brother's keeper. Indeed, otherwise his reply would be foolish. He already knew that God knew; why, then, would he lie? Why would he sink even lower by adding falsehood to crime? His very reply was an outline of his defense: he could not be judged because he did not know the law, because he was not aware of his responsibility. Now he did know, but it was too late to turn back. Abel was dead and death is as absolute as life.

Which, in the final analysis and judging by the use of the word *anokhi* (exclusive to God), means that man is responsible for his fellow-man, himself and God. What he does commits more than his own person, his own world.

A harrowing Midrash clearly attests to this. Listen to God speaking to Cain: *Kol dmei akhikha tzoakim elai min haadamah, al tikra elai ki-im alai*—The voice of your brother's blood cries out to Me from the depths of the earth. This should not be read as *to* Me but as *at* Me, *against* Me. What you have done, Cain, you have done also in My name; you have shared with Me your projects and daydreams; you have made Me responsible for your acts as I make you responsible for My creation.

And so if the first death in history enters our collective memory as a murder, it means that death itself is an injustice. Perhaps Cain killed in protest against death.

And here we see our hero in a new light: that of rebel. Thus rehabilitated, Cain would be the first idealist or nihilist revolutionary; having rebelled not against his parents but against God. Against God on behalf of his parents.

An appealing idea. I would like to believe that Cain acted out of love. To avenge his passionately beloved parents' honor, to protest their misery. He no doubt considered that God had punished them unjustly; he could see it well whenever he watched his old father and his weeping mother crushed by nostalgia. It affected him; in fact, it made him so indignant that, says the Midrash, he shouted: *Let din velet dayan*—There is neither judge nor justice in this world.

I would like to think that Cain did not rise up against his brother but against God, whose ways he found incomprehensible, intolerable. That he killed his brother to erase man's resignation and passivity. That he could not go on living as though nothing had changed and refused to

6 0

resemble Abel, who chose to ignore the outrage endured by their parents. I would like to think that Cain killed to push immanent injustice to its ultimate absurd conclusion, as if to shout to God: Is that what You wanted? Well, I shall go to the end! You don't like Your own creation? All right, I'll help You destroy it. Says the Midrash: Cain wished to restore the world to its original state of chaos.

And suddenly we *understand* Cain. A Cain tragically aware of his shortcomings, profoundly human and vulnerable. Having discovered evil and fatality in creation and in himself, having seen that man wanders down a road strewn with obstacles and traps, confronted with the inadequacy of his means and the extent of his solitude, Cain in his desperation decided to end it all immediately: better bring to an end this miserable human adventure before it begot new injustices of infinitely more frightening proportions.

Cain killed his brother—one half of mankind—out of disillusionment and perhaps out of love, weeping over all men and himself. His purpose? To destroy, to uproot creation. His reasoning? If this is man, I refuse to share his fate; if this is life, then I don't want it. Cain killed Abel, and it was only a first step. He will follow him into death. Every murder is a suicide: Cain killed Cain in Abel.

Well, that is what I would like to think.

But the text prevents us from going too far afield. Cain did not commit suicide. After his trial he settled down and his children lived and had children. Abel died for nothing; Cain killed for nothing. Their common tale is a tale of absurdity; it could not have taken place.

Then the aged Adam reappears on the scene—astounding us. By his vigor. And his daring. Despite the holocaust that had ravaged his family, he went on to become a father for the third time. Eve bore him a son and they named him Seth. How did they arrive at such a decision? In a universe that bears the seal of violence, a universe crushed by hate, what good was it to begin again? What right had they to condemn their new child to live and die?

We must assume that Adam and Eve wanted this third son out of consideration for their distant descendants. Without Seth, we would all carry an eternal burden; we would all be the heirs, if not the successors, of Cain and *only* Cain, since his brother died unwed and childless. And so the Torah releases our bonds with the assassin by putting an end to both his life and his progeny. Killed by Lemekh, Cain vanishes from the Bible; his history is cut short. Nor will the Torah mention it again. And a new chapter opens: *And here are the origins of man,* linking us to a new and different beginning. We can all, in good faith, claim Seth as our ancestor. Seth, who had no part in the drama unleashed by his brothers.

Let us come back to our original question: Was Cain guilty? We must answer yes without equivocation. Despite all and anything he may have wished to accomplish by his crime, transcending his crime, from the point of view of Jewish tradition there can be no extenuating circumstances. Did he suffer? Had God treated him unfairly? He should have told Him so. Had not God asked him the question: *Why is your face so somber?* Cain could have, should have, answered. And said what was on his mind. But he chose to remain silent, to swallow his grudge and transform it into poisonous hate. In so doing, he deprived himself of the right to judge God by killing his brother.

In fact, even if his revolt against God may have been justified, his crime will never be. For no man has the right to sacrifice his or anybody else's future. No man has the right to use another as an instrument, an abstraction. A murder is never justified, even when committed to ensure a better future. Cain may have dreamed of saving mankind from suffering, but it was Abel who paid the price.

No man is ever alone in history; every man *is* history. That is what Jewish tradition teaches us. Cain had no right to decide for us, and even less for Abel. Whoever destroys does so in the present, but his guilt remains after he is gone.

Cain may have had the world's best intentions; his may have been a pure vision. But he was wrong to deny, to repudiate, life—even his own.

If only Cain had chosen words rather than violence, if only he had turned to God and spoken to Him thus:

— Master of the Universe, lend me Your ear. You are my witness as I am Yours. You are my judge and I am afraid, I am afraid to judge. Admit though that I have had

63

every reason to cry out to You my anguish and my wrath; I have every means to oppose my injustice to Yours. Admit that I could strike my brother as You yourself punished my father. Admit that I owe it to myself to protest against the ordeals You impose on man. I could drown mankind with my tears and in its blood. I could bring this farce to an end; that may even be what You want, what You are driving me to. But I shall not do it, do You hear me, Master of the Universe, I shall not do it, I shall not destroy, do You hear me, I shall not kill!

Had Cain spoken thus, how different history would have turned out! It would not have been the desperate adventure of two brothers, one of whom asserted himself by killing and the other by letting himself be killed, but the beautiful and passionate, pure and purifying gesture of a noble and fervent mankind.

Had Cain chosen to bear witness rather than to shed blood, his fate would have become our example and our ideal, and not the symbol of our malediction. His name would evoke pride, not fear. Instead of suggesting death, he would have remained our brother.

PARABLES AND
SAYINGS II

I*t was Passover eve. Adam, who was resting with his family, turned to his two sons and said:*

— There will come a day when the children of Israel will devote this night to the celebration of their alliance with God and to commemorating their liberation; they will bring Him offerings and sacrifices. I want you to do now what they will do when that day will come.

Cain and Abel had to obey. The former offered God what he had too much of, whereas the latter parted with the best he possessed.

And God accepted Abel's gifts and rejected Cain's.

And Cain spoke to Abel and said:

— It is claimed that the world is ruled by mercy; that is false. It is also claimed that one's good deeds are taken into account; that too is false. As for me, I am telling you that the Law is distorted, disfigured by flattery, and what is

65

happening to us is irrefutable proof. You flatter God and that is why He favors you.

— Don't say that, replied Abel. God is justice and His justice is unalterable. If God has favored me, it is only because my deeds are better than yours.

— I refuse to believe this. In truth, there is no judge or justice in this world; as for the world-to-come, it does not exist.

— God is just and His truth is just, said Abel. And know that there does exist a celestial world corresponding to the one on earth. And that the just will be rewarded, just as the wicked will be punished.

It was during that conversation that Cain killed his brother, Abel.

Abel's body, guarded by his faithful sheepdog, remained for a long time among the pebbles and the weeds, exposed to the winds and the sun, while Adam and Eve stared at him and lamented; they didn't know what to do.

Until a raven who had just lost his mate decided to show them; with his beak he slowly dug a hole and gently placed his dead mate inside. Whereupon Adam declared:

— We shall do as the raven did.

And he buried his son.

But Adam remained in mourning. For one hundred and twenty-seven years he lived without joy or desire. So great was his sadness that he avoided his spouse. God had to remind him that the world was waiting to be inhabited and that life had been given to him to be transmitted. Only then did Adam and Eve draw together again.

And God said to Cain:

— Since you have repented, don't stay here any longer, you must go away.

And Cain went into exile. And everywhere he went, the ground shook under his feet as though to repudiate him. And everywhere he went, the beasts and the animals threw themselves upon him to devour him and thus to avenge the blood of Abel, their friend.

To protect him and isolate him, God marked his forehead with a sign in the shape of the sun. No, said Rabbi Nehemia: in the shape of a boil. No, said Rav: God gave him a dog to watch over him. No, said Abba Yossi: he caused a horn to grow on his forehead as a reminder to man that he is capable of both murder and repentance.

The story is told that Ashmedai, king of demons, visited King Solomon and asked:

— Would you like me to show you something you have never seen before?

Solomon said yes. Whereupon the visitor plunged his arm into time and space and brought back a man who had two heads and four eyes. Though frightened, the king invited the strange creature into his private quarters and questioned him:

— *Who are you? Whose son are you?*

— *I am Cain's descendant.*

— *Where do you live?*

— *Somewhere, in a place you call Tevel.*

— *Do you have a sun there? A moon?*

— *Certainly, said the man with the two heads and four eyes. We plow our fields. We wait for the harvest, just like you. We own cattle, just like you.*

— *And the sun, said King Solomon, on which side does it rise where you come from?*

— *It rises in the west and it sets in the east.*

— *And do you say prayers?*

— *Certainly. And they are very beautiful. We praise the Almighty for the wisdom with which He runs the universe.*

— *Would you like to stay among us or would you prefer to go home?*

— *I would like to go home.*

Whereupon King Solomon summoned Ashmedai, king of demons, and ordered him to take back to his home this descendant of Cain's. But Ashmedai shook his head and said:

— *Unfortunately, that can no longer be done; it is not in my power.*

A saying: Cain's true punishment? He unlearned the meaning of Shabbat.

THE SACRIFICE
OF ISAAC: A
SURVIVOR'S STORY

T HIS STRANGE TALE is about fear and faith, fear and defiance, fear and laughter.

Terrifying in content, it has become a source of consolation to those who, in retelling it, make it part of their own experience. Here is a story that contains Jewish destiny in its totality, just as the flame is contained in the single spark by which it comes to life. Every major theme, every passion and obsession that make Judaism the adventure that it is, can be traced back to it: man's anguish when he finds himself face to face with God, his quest for purity and purpose, the conflict of having to choose between dreams of the past and dreams of the future, between absolute faith and absolute justice, between the need to obey God's will and to rebel against it; between his yearnings for freedom and for sacrifice, his desire to justify hope and despair with words and silence—the same words and the same silence. It is all there.

69

As a literary composition, this tale—known as the *Akeda*—is unmatched in Scripture. Austere and powerful, its every word reverberates into infinity, evoking suspense and drama, uncovering a whole mood based on a before and continuing into an after, culminating in a climax which endows its characters with another dimension. They are human—and more: forceful and real despite the metaphysical implications. At every step, their condition remains relevant and of burning gravity.

This very ancient story is still our own and we shall continue to be bound to it in the most intimate way. We may not know it, but every one of us, at one time or another, is called upon to play a part in it. What part? Are we Abraham or Isaac? We are Jacob, that is to say, Israel. And Israel began with Abraham.

Let us reread the text.

Once upon a time there lived a man for all seasons, blessed with all talents and virtues, deserving of every grace. His name was Abraham and his mission was to serve as God's messenger among men too vain and blind to recognize His glory. Tradition rates him higher than Moses—whose Law he observed; higher even than Adam —whose errors he was asked to correct.

Abraham: the first enemy of idolatry. The first angry young man. The first rebel to rise up against the "establishment," society and authority. The first to demystify official taboos and suspend ritual prohibitions. The first to reject civilization in order to form a minority of one. The first believer, the first one to suffer for his belief. Alone against the world, he declared himself free. Alone against the world, he braved the fire and the mob, affirming that God is one and present wherever His name is invoked; that one is the secret and the beginning of all that exists in heaven and on earth and that God's secret coincides with that of man.

And yet. Notwithstanding his total faith in God and His justice, His kindness as well, he did not for a moment hesitate to take God to task as he tried to save two condemned cities from destruction: How can You—who embody justice—be unjust? He was the first who dared query God. And God listened and answered. For unlike Job, Abraham was protesting on behalf of others, not of himself. God forgave Abraham everything, including his questions. God is God and Abraham was His faithful servant; one was sure of the other. To test his will and vision, God had made him leave the security of his father's home, challenge rulers and engage their armies in battle, endure hunger and exile, disgrace and fire. His trust in God was never shaken. So loyal was he to God that he was rewarded with a son who became symbol and bearer of grace and benediction for generations to come.

Then one day God decided once more to test him—for the tenth and last time: Take your son and bring him to Me as an offering. The term used is *ola,* which means an offering that has been totally consumed, a holocaust. And Abraham complied. Without an argument. Without ques-

71

tioning or even trying to understand, without trying to stall. Without a word to anyone, not even his wife Sarah, without a tear; he simply waited for the next morning and left the house before she awakened. He saddled his donkey, and accompanied by his son and two servants, started on the road to Mount Moriah. After a three-day journey —which according to Kierkegaard lasted longer than the four thousand years separating us from the event—father and son left the servants and donkey behind and began their ascent of the mountain. When they reached the top they erected an altar and prepared for the ritual. Everything was ready: the wood, the knife, the fire. Slaughterer and victim looked into each other's eyes and for one moment all of creation held its breath. The same fear penetrated the father and the son. A Midrash describes Isaac's fear. Stretched out on the altar, his wrists and ankles bound, Isaac saw the Temple in Jerusalem first destroyed and then rebuilt, and at the moment of the supreme test, Isaac understood that what was happening to him would happen to others, that this was to be a tale without an end, an experience to be endured by his children and theirs. Never would they be spared the torture. The father's anguish, on the other hand, was not linked to the future; by sacrificing his son to obey God's will, Abraham knew that he was, in fact, sacrificing his knowledge *of* God and his faith *in* Him. If Isaac were to die, to whom would the father transmit this faith, this knowledge? The end of Isaac would connote the end of a prodigious adventure: the first would become the last. One cannot conceive of a more crushing or more devastating anguish: I shall thus have lived, suffered and caused others to suffer for nothing.

And the miracle took place. Death was defeated, the tragedy averted. The blade that could have cut the line—and prevented Israel from being born—was halted, suspended.

Was thus the mystery resolved? Hardly. As one plunges into Midrashic literature, one feels its poignancy. It leaves one troubled. The question is no longer whether Isaac was saved but whether the miracle could happen again. And how often. And for what reasons. And at what cost.

As a child, I read and reread this tale, my heart beating wildly; I felt dark apprehension come over me and carry me far away.

There was no understanding the three characters. Why would God, the merciful Father, demand that Abraham become inhuman, and why would Abraham accept? And Isaac, why did he submit so meekly? Not having received a direct order to let himself be sacrificed, why did he consent?

I could not understand. If God needs human suffering to be God, how can man foresee an end to that suffering? And if faith in God must result in self-denial, how can faith claim to elevate and improve man?

These were painful questions, especially for an adoles-

73

cent, because they did not fit into the framework of the sin-punishment concept, to which all religious thought had accustomed us. The only exception is one Midrash, which asks: Why was Abraham tested on Mount Moriah? And it answers: Because he favored his son Isaac over his eldest, Ishmael. This hypothesis has the merit of "justifying" the order that Abraham received from God and which otherwise would seem incomprehensible. Let us reread the command. God told Abraham: *Kakh na eth binkha eth yekhidkha asher ahavta eth Yitzhak*—Take your son, your only son, whom you love, Isaac, and bring him to Me in holocaust. Only son? But that's a mistake! What about Ishmael? Forgotten by Abraham, was he equally forgotten by God? To introduce the possibility of guilt of the father toward his eldest son—a guilt that carries its own punishment—we have but to change the emphasis of the sentence: *Kakh na eth binkha*—Take your son, comma, *eth yekhidkha asher ahavta,* the only one that you love, Isaac, and bring him to Me: I want him as an expiatory sacrifice. The term *yekhidkha*—the only one —would no longer be contrary to the facts.

But we are not here concerned with punctuation or even with immanent morality. Had it been a simple matter of expiating a sin or an injustice, the sacrifice would not have been so exceptional a test: in those days this kind of immolation was current practice among the peoples of the region.

Even were we to assume for a moment that God wished to punish a sinful father, why would he inflict a worse—

and supreme—punishment on the son? Abraham could have asked the question, he could have spoken up just as he had done when trying to save Sodom and Gomorrah. Why didn't he? According to the Midrash, he knew and observed the laws and commandments of Torah; didn't he know that by killing, he would mutilate the very image of God? Didn't he know, he who knew everything, didn't he know that in Jewish tradition God is bound to obey His own Law, including the most urgent of all: Thou shalt not kill! Or should we imagine a more human motivation for Abraham's strange behavior? The repressed resentment of a father toward a son who will survive him? Or else man's need to kill that which he loves?

To me the *Akeda* was an unfathomable mystery given to every generation, to be relived, if not solved—one of the great mysteries of our history, a mystery so opaque that it obscures not only the facts but also the names of the protagonists.

Why did Abraham, the would-be slaughterer, become, in our prayers, the symbol of *hesed:* grace, compassion and love? A symbol of love, he who was ready to throttle his son?

And Isaac, why was he called Isaac? *Yitzhak?* He who will laugh? Laugh at whom? At what? Or, as Sarah thought, he who will make others laugh? Why was the most tragic figure in Biblical history given such a bizarre name?

• • •

75

Throughout the centuries, hundreds of volumes have been written on the *Akeda,* a term recalling the fact that Isaac was *bound* to the altar, and mistakenly translated as "sacrifice" of Isaac.

In passing, we should mention the role played by this scene in Christianity: the threat hanging over Isaac is seen as a prefiguration of the crucifixion. Except that on Mount Moriah the act was *not* consummated: the father did *not* abandon his son. Such is the distance between Moriah and Golgotha. In Jewish tradition man cannot use death as a means of glorifying God. Every man is an end unto himself, a living eternity; no man has the right to sacrifice another, not even to God. Had he killed his son, Abraham would have become the forefather of a people—but not the Jewish people. For the Jew, all truth must spring from life, never from death. To us, crucifixion represents not a step forward but a step backward: at the top of Moriah, the living remains alive, thus marking the end of an era of ritual murder. To invoke the *Akeda* is tantamount to calling for mercy—whereas from the beginning Golgotha has served as pretext for countless massacres of sons and fathers cut down together by sword and fire in the name of a word that considered itself synonymous with love.

Let us now close the parentheses. And follow Abraham.

What do we know about his life and his person? Many things told to us by the Bible and expounded upon by the Midrash. We are treated to an abundance of precise and picturesque details on both his private and public activities. We are informed about his habits, his moods, his business relationships, his difficulties with his neighbors, his servants and his concubines. He was rich, hospitable, friendly and giving; he invited strangers into his home without asking who they were or what the purpose of their visit might be. He welcomed the hungry and helped the poor, angels and beggars alike, offering them both shelter and food.

The Midrash is intent on stressing that his physical prowess was considerable. He was brave to the point of temerity, never shunning a battle. He lost only one, and that was due only to the adversary's overwhelming numerical superiority: forty-five thousand commanders, eighty thousand heroic warriors and sixty thousand soldiers had to combine forces to subdue him. He was powerful and feared, and so it was only natural that he should marry the most beautiful woman in the world. He often took her along on his journeys, and it is interesting to note that once, on arriving in Egypt, he introduced her . . . as his sister.

He evidently was a restless man who could not stay idle long. He was forever seeking new stimulation, new certainties; he abhorred all routine. He would go from Haran to Canaan, sometimes pushing as far as Damascus, in his search for worthy adversaries. He was an explorer of some stature who affronted kings and robbers, and enjoyed defeating them, exulting when he broke their pride.

Yet his greatest adventure was his encounter with God

—an encounter which was a result of deliberate choice on both sides. They addressed one another as equals. According to the Midrash, God said to Abraham: *Ani yekhidi veata yekhidi*—I am alone and you are alone, alone to know and proclaim it. From that moment on, their dialogue took place under the implacable sign of the absolute: they were to be both partners and accomplices. Before, says legend, God reigned only in heaven; it was Abraham who extended his rule unto the earth.

Since clearly an interlocutor of God's could not be a man of mediocrity, the Midrash confers upon Abraham a boundless wealth of titles and virtues: his were the powers of a sovereign ruler, the wisdom of a Just Man, the fiery language of a prophet or high priest. He spoke every tongue and mastered every art; he had access to secrets no living man before him had ever glimpsed, much less understood.

Why was he given the surname *Haivri,* the Hebrew? *Ivri,* says one source, comes from the word *ever,* which means "side": Abraham stood on one side and the whole world on the other. According to another explanation, not without humor, Abraham was nicknamed the Hebrew simply because, with God, he . . . conversed in Hebrew.

And one begins to wonder, since God and he loved one another so much and collaborated so closely, why these tests? Why these ordeals and torture? Because God tests only the strong. The weak do not resist or resist poorly; they are of no consequence. But then, what good is it to resist, since God knows the outcome in advance? Answer: God knows, man does not.

Most commentators assume that Abraham was tested for his own good. To serve as an example to the peoples of the world and to earn him their leaders' reverence. And also to harden him; to awaken in him an awareness of his own strength and potential.

Of course, this does not satisfy everyone: the idea that suffering is good for Jews is one that owes its popularity to our enemies.

And indeed there is another explanation, though not a very original one, that brings into the picture an old acquaintance, always present in moments of crisis and doubt: Satan. Source of all evil, supreme temptor. The easy, glib answer, the scapegoat. The crafty gambler, the unabashed liar. The servant who conveniently carries out the Master's dirty work, accepting all blame and anathema in His place. The sacrifice of Isaac? God had nothing to do with it; it was all Satan's doing. God did not want this test; Satan demanded it. The inhuman game was Satan's scheme and he bears full responsibility. Satan: the ideal alibi.

Just as he did with Job—who is frequently compared to Abraham for more than one reason—Satan used gossip to distort and embellish history. On his return from an inspection tour on earth, he handed his report to the Almighty while telling Him his impressions. Thus he came to his surprise visit with Abraham, who was celebrating the birth of his beloved son Isaac. Rejoicing, sumptuous meals, public festivities, Satan did not spare the superlatives, as usual. And do You know, said he perfidiously, do You know that Your faithful servant Abraham has forgotten You—You? Yes indeed, his good fortune has gone to his head; he forgot to set aside an offering for You. He thought only of his joy, as though it did not come from You; he fed all his guests, yet he neglected to offer You the youngest of his sheep, if only as a modest token of his gratitude. God was not convinced. He answered: No, no, you're wrong to suspect My faithful Abraham; he is devoted to Me, he loves Me, he would give Me all that he possesses—he would give me his son were I to ask him. Really? said Satan. Are You sure? I'm not. And God was provoked and felt compelled to accept the challenge. The rest can be found in Scripture.

The Biblical narrative is of exemplary purity of line, sobriety and terseness. Not one superfluous word, not one useless gesture. The imagery is striking, the language austere, the dialogue so incisive, it leaves one with a knot in one's throat.

. . . *And, some time afterward, God put Abraham to the test. He said to him: Abraham. And he answered: Here I am. And He said: Take your son, your favored one, Isaac, whom you love, and go to the land of Moriah and offer him there as a burnt offering on one of the heights which I will point out to you.*

This time Abraham did not answer: *Here I am;* he did not answer at all. He went home, lay down and fell asleep.

The next morning he rose, awakened his son and two of his servants, and started out on his journey. At the end of three days—at the end of a silence that lasted three days —he saw the appointed place in the distance. He halted, and instructed the servants: *You stay here with the ass. The boy and I will go up there; we will worship and we will return to you.*

Abraham took the wood for the burnt offering and gave it to his son, Isaac. He himself took the firestone and the knife; and the two walked away together.

The last sentence gives us the key: one went to face death, the other to give it, but they went together; still close to one another though everything already separated them. God was waiting for them and they were going toward Him together. But then Isaac, who until that moment had not opened his mouth, turned to his father and uttered a single word: *Father.* And for the second time Abraham answered: *Here I am.* Was it because of the silence that followed this painfully hushed affirmation? Isaac began to feel uneasy; he wanted to be reassured or at least understand.

And Isaac said: Here is the firestone and the wood; but where is the sheep for the burnt offering?

Embarrassed, suddenly shy, Abraham tried to equivocate: *God will see to the sheep for His burnt offering, my son. And the two of them walked on together.*

The march continued. The two of them alone in the world, encircled by God's unfathomable design. But they were *together.* Now the repetition renders a new sound while adding to the dramatic intensity of the narrative.

And Isaac began to guess, to understand. And then he knew. And the father and the son remained united. Together they reached the top of the mountain; together they erected the altar; together they prepared the wood and the fire. Everything was ready, nothing was missing. And Isaac lay on the altar, silently gazing at his father.

And Abraham picked up the knife to slay his son. Then an angel of the Lord called to him from heaven: Abraham, Abraham! And he answered: Here I am.

For the third time he answered: *Here I am.* I am the same, the same person who answered Your first call; I answer Your call, whatever its nature; and even were *it* to change, *I* would not.

And the angel said: Do not raise your hand against the boy or do anything to him. For now I know that you fear God, since you have not withheld your son, your favored one, from Me.

All is well that ends well. The sacrifice took place, yet Isaac remained alive: a ram was slaughtered and burned in his stead. Abraham reconciled himself with his conscience. And the angel, exulting, renewed before him shining promises for the future: his children, as numerous as the stars reflected in the sea, would inherit the earth. Abraham once more plunged into the magnificent dream which would always remind him of his covenant with God. No, the future was not dead. No, truth would not be stifled. No, exile would not go on indefinitely. Abraham should have returned home a happy and serene man. Except that the tale ends with a strange sentence which opens rather than heals the wounds: *Vayashav avraham el nearav* —And Abraham returned to his servants. Note the singular: *Vayashav,* he returned. He, Abraham. Alone. And Isaac? Where was Isaac? Why was he not with his father? What had happened to him? Are we to understand that father and son were no longer together? That the experience they just shared had separated them—albeit only *after* the event? That Isaac, unlike Abraham, was no longer the same person, that the real Isaac remained there, on the altar?

These profoundly disquieting questions provoked passionate responses in the Midrash, where the theme of the *Akeda* occupies as important a place as the creation of the world or the revelation at Sinai.

The Midrash, in this case, does not limit itself to stating the facts and commenting upon them. It delves into the very heart and silence of the cast of characters. It examines them from every angle; it follows them into their innermost selves; it goes so far as to imagine the unimaginable.

The prologue is focused on a single character: Abraham. He alone knew what was about to happen. To his wife he said: We are going to pray. To his son he said: We shall study and meditate. The secret was his alone; he alone knew there was a secret—and he refused to share it.

Sarah and Isaac barely participated in the drama as it unfolded. They were there but their presence is not sustained. As for God, He was present only by virtue of Abraham's lie. We know that He was present, watching, listening, waiting; we know it because Abraham lied for Him, because Abraham hid his fear and grief from Him. What would Abraham do? Which side would he choose? God's or the victim's? Someone knew the answer. Sarah and Isaac did not even know the question. Not yet. But Satan did. At that moment he seems to have been closer to God than man.

With his appearance on stage, the drama gains in suspense. Still, his behavior seems irrational. Having suggested—no, demanded—Isaac's sacrifice, he now abruptly did his utmost to prevent it. Having tried—successfully—to influence God, he now tried to influence Abraham.

Let us listen to the Midrash:

As Abraham journeyed toward Moriah, an old man appeared before him. It was Satan in disguise. He asked: Where are you going? — To prayer, said Abraham. — With a knife? With a firestone and wood? Nobody goes to prayer like that. — Well, Abraham explained, we may be delayed a day or two. We then would have to slaughter a lamb, place it on a fire to feed ourselves; it is best to be prepared. — Thereupon Satan dropped his mask and said: Poor old man with your poor old tales! Do you think you can fool me? Don't you know I was present when the order was given? — Abraham did not reply. — Satan continued shouting: Tell me, old man, have you lost your

8 4

mind, have you emptied your heart of all human feeling? Will you really sacrifice your son, given to you at the age of one hundred? — Yes, said Abraham, I shall. — But tomorrow, old fool, He will demand more sacrifices, more cruel yet; will you be able to perform them too? — I hope so, replied Abraham. I hope to always be able to obey Him. — But tomorrow, poor mortal, He may accuse you of murder, He who issued the order! He will condemn you for having killed your son, He will condemn you for having obeyed! Will you do it nevertheless? — Yes, I shall, Abraham insisted, I shall do it anyway. I must obey Him, that is my desire.

Having failed with the father, Satan tried his luck with the son. He appeared before him disguised as a young boy: Where are you going? — To study Torah, answered Isaac. — Now or after your death? — What a foolish question, said Isaac. Of course now. Don't you know the Torah is given only to the living? — Poor son of a poor woman, said Satan. For years and years she lived in hope and prayer to give birth to you, and now this old man, your own father, has gone mad. Look at him, he is going to kill you! Isaac would not believe him; instead he looked at his father with love. So Satan went on, feigning compassion: Yes, you are about to die, believe me. And do you know who will rejoice? Your brother Ishmael. He will be happy. Your clothes, your possessions, the gifts meant for you, he will get them all. — This argument, so childish, so human, gave Isaac pause. He turned to his father and shyly asked him: Look at this person, Father. Listen to what he

85

says. — Don't pay any attention, son, said Abraham. His words are empty of meaning and truth. Do not listen.

Still, the story does not end here. Satan refused to concede defeat. He invented other obstacles. He turned himself into a river; Abraham chased the waves away. He then changed himself into a cloud, only to be dispersed by Abraham. Finally Satan had a brilliant idea. He would use the most dangerous weapon of all: truth. He decided to gamble, to reveal the facts, and declared: Abraham, this is what I have heard backstage, up there: ultimately the lamb will be the offering; the lamb and not Isaac. Do you hear me, old man: you have nothing to fear, neither does Isaac. Whether you continue or turn back, it will all be the same. It is nothing but a game, a simple test. So stop tormenting yourself and taking yourself for a hero.

Had Abraham believed Satan—who was, after all, telling the truth—the drama would have ended then and there. Instead he ignored Satan and proceeded with his now silent march toward that precise point where despair and faith were to meet in a fiery and senseless quest.

As always in the Midrash, these parables reflect the dramatic demands of the narrative. Through them, internal conflicts become tangible, visible.

Because we are allowed to see Satan and Isaac's awareness of his presence, we realize more fully Abraham's loneliness. Satan personifies the doubt Abraham *had* to have in order to remain human. The same is true for Isaac's fear. Had Isaac remained blind to the end, silent and confident to the last minute, his conduct would have seemed naïve rather than innocent, childish rather than brave. One Midrash tells us that he was, in fact, thirty-seven years old at that time. At a certain point he had to understand, had to realize that the man walking next to him was acting out a role other than that of father. By becoming afraid, he became human and a child once more. One text goes so far as to insinuate that father and son walked toward Moriah hand in hand because Abraham wished to prevent Isaac from taking flight, for Isaac was afraid.

Satan himself became human. Having abused truth in vain, he lost his head. Unable to accept defeat, he set out to devise another scheme, as we shall see later. For the moment let us continue our examination of Abraham's behavior. He refused to believe Satan—how could he be so sure that he was not wrong? And what if Satan had been telling the truth? By revealing the real future—the actual outcome—Satan had admitted that in fact he, Satan, had been the one who had demanded and obtained the sacrifice of Isaac: and what if it were not a lie? For Abraham, that was the essence of the problem, the true anguish: to die for God is conceivable; it is even conceivable, in certain extraordinary and extreme situations, that one may accept to provoke death for God. But for Satan?

Yet Abraham did not hesitate. He knew. He knew that between divine tests and the others, there is a difference both in substance and form; certain signs are unmistakable. Satan aims to make things easier, God does not. It was enough for Abraham to ask himself which would be the

8 7

easier way. Surely it would be easier to go back home with a light heart and a good conscience, and reassure Sarah, who certainly would be worrying by now. Therefore, he had to do the opposite. He continued his march without as much as a glance backward. It definitely was a deliberate choice; the Midrash stresses that point by explaining why the march lasted three days. So that people would not say that father and son had acted in a state of shock.

No. Both were perfectly lucid and aware, in control of their senses. They had time to prepare themselves, to think, to consider alternatives, to imagine the event in all its horror.

On the morning of the third day, says the Midrash, Abraham could distinguish the appointed place from afar —just as the people did later before Sinai. He turned to his son and asked: Do you see what I see? Yes, replied Isaac, I see a splendid mountain under a cloud of fire. Then Abraham turned to his two servants and asked: And you, what do you see? The servants, passive onlookers, saw nothing but the desert. And Abraham understood that the event did not concern them and that they were to stay behind. And that the place was indeed the place.

And so the father and the son walked away together— *ze laakod veze léaked,* the one to bind and the other to be bound, *ze lishkhot veze lishakhet,* the one to slaughter and the other to be slaughtered—sharing the same allegiance to the same God, responding to the same call. The sacrifice was to be their joint offering; father and son had never before been so close. The Midrashic text emphasizes this, as if to show another tragic aspect of the *Akeda,* namely, the equation between Abraham and Isaac. Abraham and Isaac were equals, in spite of their opposing roles as victim and executioner. But Abraham himself, whose victim was he? God's? Once more the key word is *yakhdav,* together: victims together. Together they gathered the wood, together they arranged it on the altar, together they set the stage for the drama to unfold. Abraham, says the text, behaved like a happy father preparing to celebrate his son's wedding, and Isaac like a groom about to meet his bride-to-be. Both were serene, at peace with themselves and each other.

But then, suddenly, for a brief moment, Isaac reentered reality and grasped the magnitude and horror of what was to come: Father, what will you do, Mother and you, afterward? — He who has consoled us until now, answered Abraham, will continue to console us. — Father, Isaac went on after a silence, I am afraid, afraid of being afraid. You must bind me securely. And a little later: Father, when you shall speak to my mother, when you shall tell her, make sure she is not standing near the well or on the roof, lest she fall and hurt herself.

Our attention thereafter is centered on Isaac stretched out on the altar. We watch him as Abraham gazes straight into his eyes. Abraham was weeping, his tears streaming into the eyes of his son, leaving a scar never to be erased. So bitterly did he weep that his knife slipped from his hands and fell to the ground. Only then, not before, did he shout in despair, and only then did God part the heavens and allow Isaac to see the higher sanctuaries of the *merkava,* of creation, with entire rows of angels lamenting: *Yakhid shokhet veyakhid nishkat*—Look at the slaughterer, he is alone and so is the one he is about to slaughter. All the worlds in all the spheres were in tumult: Isaac had become the center of the universe. He could not be allowed to die, not now, not like this. And die he would not. The voice of an angel was heard: Do not raise your hand against the boy, Abraham. Isaac must live.

Why did an angel intervene rather than God Himself? The Midrash answers: God alone may order death, but to save a human life, an angel is enough.

A profoundly generous and beautiful explanation, but I have another which I prefer. Mine allows me to do what until now I could not; namely, to identify not only with Isaac but also with Abraham.

The time has come for the storyteller to confess that he has always felt much closer to Isaac than to his father, Abraham.

I have never really been able to accept the idea that inhumanity could be one more way for man to move closer to God. Kierkegaard's too convenient theory of occasional "ethical suspension" never appealed to me. Kierkegaard maintains that Abraham concealed Isaac's fate from him in order to protect his faith in God; let Isaac lose faith in man rather than in man's Creator. These are concepts rejected by Jewish tradition. God's Law—we said it earlier

—commits God as well; but while God cannot suspend His law, it is given to man—to man and not to God—to interpret it. However, faith in God is linked to faith in man, and one cannot be separated from the other.

Let us once again examine the question: Why didn't Abraham tell Isaac the truth? Because he thought the *Akeda* was a matter strictly between himself and God; it concerned nobody else, not even Isaac.

Thus I place my trust in man's strength. God does not like man to come to him through resignation. Man must strive to reach God through knowledge and love. God loves man to be clear-sighted and outspoken, not blindly obsequious. He respected Job because he dared to stand up to Him. Abraham had interceded on behalf of the two sinful cities long before the test with Isaac.

A double-edged test. God subjected Abraham to it, yet at the same time Abraham forced it on God. As though Abraham had said: I defy You, Lord. I shall submit to Your will, but let us see whether You shall go to the end, whether You shall remain passive and remain silent when the life of my son—who is also Your son—is at stake!

And God changed his mind and relented. Abraham won. That was why God sent an angel to revoke the order and congratulate him; He Himself was too embarrassed.

And suddenly we have another *coup de théâtre.* Abraham never ceases to astonish us: having won the round, he became demanding. Since God had given in, Abraham was not going to be satisfied with one victory and continue their relationship as though nothing had changed. His turn had come to dictate conditions, or else . . . he would pick up the knife—and come what may!

Let us listen to the Midrash:

When Abraham heard the angel's voice, he did not cry out with joy or express his gratitude. On the contrary, he began to argue. He, who until now had obeyed with sealed lips, suddenly showed inordinate skepticism. He questioned the counterorder he had been hoping and waiting for. First he asked that the angel identify himself in due form. Then he demanded proof that he was God's messenger, not Satan's. And finally he simply refused to accept the message, saying: God Himself ordered me to sacrifice my son, it is up to Him to rescind that order without an intermediary. And, says the Midrash, God had to give in again: He Himself finally had to tell Abraham not to harm his son.

This was Abraham's second victory; yet he was still not satisfied.

Listen . . .

When Abraham heard the celestial voice ordering him to spare his son Isaac, he declared: I swear I shall not leave the altar, Lord, before I speak my mind. — Speak, said God. — Did You not promise me that my descendants would be as numerous as the stars in the sky? — Yes, I did promise you that. — And whose descendants will they be? Mine? Mine alone? — No, said God, they will be Isaac's as well. — And didn't You also promise me that they would inherit the earth? — Yes, I promised you that too. — And whose descendants will they be? Mine alone?

— No, said God's voice, they will be Isaac's as well. — Well then, my Lord, said Abraham unabashedly, I could have pointed out to You before that Your order contradicted Your promise. I could have spoken up, I didn't. I contained my grief and held my tongue. In return, I want You to make me the following promise: that when, in the future, my children and my children's children throughout the generations will act against Your law and against Your will, You will also say nothing and forgive them. — So be it, God agreed. Let them but retell this tale and they will be forgiven.

We now begin to understand why Abraham's name has become synonymous with *hesed*. For indeed he was charitable, not so much with Isaac as with God. He could have accused Him and proved Him wrong; he didn't. By saying yes—almost to the end—he established his faith in God and His mercy, thus bringing Him closer to His creation. He won and—so says the Midrash—God loves to be defeated by His children.

But unlike God, Satan hates to lose. Unlike God, he takes revenge, however and against whomever he can. Defeated by Abraham and Isaac, he turned against Sarah, appearing before her disguised as Isaac. And he told her the *true* story that was taking place on Mount Moriah. He told her of the march, the ritual ceremony, the heavenly intervention. Barely had Satan finished talking, when Sarah fell to the ground. Dead.

Why this legend? It has a meaning. Abraham thought that the *Akeda* was a matter between himself and God, or perhaps between himself and his son. He was wrong. There is an element of the unknown in every injustice, in every adventure involving total commitment. One imposes suffering on a friend, a son, in order to win who knows what battles, to prove who knows what theories, and in the end someone else pays the price—and that someone is almost always innocent. Once the injustice has been committed, it eludes our control. All things considered, Abraham was perhaps wrong in obeying, or even in making believe that he was obeying. By including Isaac in an equation he could not comprehend, by playing with Isaac's suffering, he became unwittingly an accomplice in his wife's death.

Another text, even more cruel, goes further yet. It hints that the tragic outcome could, after all, not be averted. Hence the use of the singular verb: *Vayashav avraham el nearav.* Yes, Abraham did return alone. One does not play such games with impunity.

Of course, this hypothesis has been rejected by tradition. The ancient commentators preferred to imagine Isaac shaken but alive, spending the unaccounted-for years at a yeshiva or perhaps even in paradise, but eventually returning home.

Yet popular imagination—collective memory—adheres rather to the tragic interpretation of the text. Isaac did not accompany his father on the way back because the divine intervention came too late. The act had been consummated. Neither God nor Abraham emerged victorious from the contest. They were both losers. Hence God's pangs of guilt on Rosh Hashana, when He judges man and his deeds. Because of the drama that took place at Mount Moriah, He understands man better. Because of Abraham and Isaac, He knows that it is possible to push some endeavors too far.

That is why the theme and term of the *Akeda* have been used, throughout the centuries, to describe the destruction and disappearance of countless Jewish communities everywhere. All the pogroms, the crusades, the persecutions, the slaughters, the catastrophes, the massacres by sword and the liquidations by fire—each time it was Abraham leading his son to the altar, to the holocaust all over again.

Of all the Biblical tales, the one about Isaac is perhaps the most timeless and most relevant to our generation. We have known Jews who, like Abraham, witnessed the death of their children; who, like Isaac, lived the *Akeda* in their flesh; and some who went mad when they saw their father disappear on the altar, with the altar, in a blazing fire whose flames reached into the highest of heavens.

We have known Jews—ageless Jews—who wished to become blind for having seen God and man opposing one another in the invisible sanctuary of the celestial spheres, a sanctuary illuminated by the gigantic flames of the holocaust.

• • •

But the story does not end there. Isaac survived; he had no choice. He had to make something of his memories, his experience, in order to force us to hope.

For our survival is linked to his. Satan could kill Sarah, he could even hurt Abraham, but Isaac was beyond his reach. Isaac too represents defiance. Abraham defied God, Isaac defied death.

What did happen to Isaac after he left Mount Moriah? He became a poet—author of the *Minha* service—and did not break with society. Nor did he rebel against life. Logically, he should have aspired to wandering, to the pursuit of oblivion. Instead he settled on his land, never to leave it again, retaining his name. He married, had children, refusing to let fate turn him into a bitter man. He felt neither hatred nor anger toward his contemporaries who did not share his experience. On the contrary, he liked them and showed concern for their well-being. After Moriah, he devoted his life and his right to immortality to the defense of his people.

At the end of time, say our sages, God will tell Abraham: Your children have sinned. And Abraham will reply: Let them die to sanctify Your name. Then God will turn to Jacob and say: Your children have sinned. And Jacob will reply: Let them die to sanctify Your name. Then God will speak to Isaac: Your children have sinned. And Isaac will answer: *My* children? Are they not also Yours? Yours as well?

It will be Isaac's privilege to remain Israel's *Melitz-Yosher,* the defender of his people, pleading its cause with great ability. He will be entitled to say anything he likes to God, ask anything of Him. Because he suffered? No. Suffering, in Jewish tradition, confers no privileges. It all depends on what one makes of that suffering. Isaac knew how to transform it into prayer and love rather than into rancor and malediction. This is what gives him rights and powers no other man possesses. His reward? The Temple was built on Moriah. Not on Sinai.

Let us return to the question we asked at the beginning: Why was the most tragic of our ancestors named Isaac, a name which evokes and signifies laughter? Here is why. As the first survivor, he had to teach us, the future survivors of Jewish history, that it is possible to suffer and despair an entire lifetime and still not give up the art of laughter.

Isaac, of course, never freed himself from the traumatizing scenes that violated his youth; the holocaust had marked him and continued to haunt him forever. Yet he remained capable of laughter. And in spite of everything, he did laugh.

PARABLES AND
SAYINGS III

*A*nd *God said to Abraham:* Have no fear, I shall protect you; great will be your reward.

This verse, coming as it does after the description of Abraham's resounding victories over the kings of the region, puzzled our sages. Why did God have to reassure Abraham, who was reputed to be invincible?

Because Abraham feared the consequences of his victory, said Rabbi Levi. He was concerned lest the slain kings' sons join forces to attack him. Hence God had to reassure him: Don't be afraid, Abraham; even were all the kings in the world to unite against you, no harm would come to you, for I shall deal with them Myself.

Another explanation: Abraham was beset by doubts— how was he to know whether among the warriors he had slain, there had not been one just man who did not deserve such a death? Thus God had to dispel his fears: You have but pulled out the thorns from the king's garden; great will be your reward.

• • •

Sodom: city of sin, exuding crime, spreading evil. Punished for its deeds, not against God but against mankind. Against the weak, the destitute, the homeless, the wretched.

Said Rabbi Yehuda: In Sodom there existed a law decreeing capital punishment for anyone offering bread to a stranger, a beggar, a pauper.

And yet, when Abraham learned that God was preparing to destroy Sodom, he came to its defense. He pleaded for divine mercy, saying: If You want only this world to survive, then there can be no Law; if You want only the Law to survive, then there can be no world. You are holding the stick by both ends. Choose one or the other. Be less demanding, less intransigent, otherwise nothing will remain. Thus, according to Rabbi Levi, did Abraham plead for the city whose men devoured one another.

Three years after he drove Ishmael out of his house, Abraham, who never stopped loving him, went to visit him in the desert. A woman received him: Aissa, Ishmael's Moabite wife. Abraham asked her: Where is your husband? — Gone to harvest fruit. — I am thirsty, I am hungry, said Abraham; the journey has exhausted me. Please give me some water, a piece of bread. Aissa refused. Whereupon Abraham said to her: When your husband returns, tell him that an old man came to see him from the land of Canaan and that this old man wishes him to know that he did not like the threshold of his home. Aissa transmitted the mes-

*sage to Ishmael, who immediately repudiated her. His new
wife, Fatima, came from Egypt.*

*Three years later Abraham came back. Where is your
husband? he asked Fatima. — Gone to take care of the
camels. — I am thirsty, I am hungry, said Abraham; the
journey has made me tired. — Come inside and rest, said
Fatima, offering him bread and water. — When your husband returns, said Abraham, smiling, tell him that an old
man came to see him from the land of Canaan and that he
very much liked the threshold of his house.*

*From afar, father and son never ceased loving one an-
other.*

*To prevent the sacrifice of Isaac, Satan transformed him-
self into a river flowing across the road toward Moriah,
hoping that Abraham and his son would be unable to cross
it. As the waters reached his chin, Abraham gazed at heaven
and said: Master of the Universe, when You chose me, You
told me that You were alone just as I was alone and that
it was through me that You would make Yourself known,
and that I was to give You my son in sacrifice. But if I were
to drown, or Isaac, who would accomplish Your will? And
who would spread Your name?*

*The next moment there was not a trace left of a river on
the road to Mount Moriah.*

And Abraham sacrificed the ram in place of his son . . .
Poor ram, said certain sages. God tests man and the ram

is killed. That is unjust; after all, he has done nothing.

Said Rabbi Yehoshua: This ram had been living in paradise since the sixth day of creation, waiting to be called. He was destined from the very beginning to replace Isaac on the altar.

A special ram, with a unique destiny, of whom Rabbi Hanina ben Dossa said: Nothing of this sacrifice was lost. The ashes were dispersed in the Temple's sanctuary; the sinews David used as cords for his harp; the skin was claimed by the prophet Elijah to clothe himself; as for the two horns, the smaller one called the people together at the foot of Mount Sinai and the larger one will resound one day, announcing the coming of the Messiah.

One day Mikha, the king of the Moabites, summoned his personal counselors and asked them: Wherein lies the strength of the Jewish people? Why do we not succeed in destroying it? — Its strength lies in Abraham, replied the counselors. — Abraham, Abraham, who is he? — Their ancestor, the first of their patriarchs. — But whatever did he do to deserve such power? asked the king. — Abraham was ready to sacrifice his son to God, replied the counselors. — And did he do it? — No, it was only a test. — Then I shall do better and be more powerful than he.

And the Moabite king ordered the arrest of more than one man, more than ten men, more than a hundred men and sacrificed them all to his gods. And he felt his strength ebbing. He died without having understood.

. . .

Rabbi Hanan, son of Rava, said in the name of Rav: The day Abraham gave up his soul, all the kings and all the mighty princes of the world gathered to mourn him, crying together: Woe to the world that has lost its guide, woe to the vessel that has lost its captain.

AND JACOB FOUGHT
THE ANGEL

A MAN, A DREAM, A STORY.

We know the place. We know the story. We know some
of the characters, not all. As we try to gain deeper understanding, to grasp them in their human, albeit sometimes
unreal, truth, we realize that one of them eludes us; we do
not even know his name.

At first glance, what we seem to be dealing with here are
solitude and prayer, struggle and survival, victory and
defeat. But as we take a closer look we see that the story,
with its part of mystery, is dominated by shadow.

A solitary man, an incandescent dream, a conflict.
Two brothers, two destinies. Linked and separated by
night.

The place: somewhere in this distant land which today
we call Jordan. Jacob called it Mahanaim, the site where

1 0 3

he divided his people into two groups so that if one were to perish, the other might survive.

A man facing death, a man imagining his future.

In the distance, muffled sounds from some caravan settling down to rest after the fatigue and strains of the journey. This had not been an easy journey but rather like a flight without end or beginning. Along the way the enemy had changed from the cheated father-in-law determined to recover his property, to the irate enemy brother drunk with vengeance. And, strangely, the man—Jacob—chose to run to meet him, rather than run away.

It was dark. Anxious, ominous silence hung over the plain. No sound except the rustling of the Jabbok stream, eager to throw itself into the sea and tell the shadows met here and there the incredible story of this man determined to remain behind alone, for the last time alone in the night and alone in the plain, as though he were waiting for someone, a mysterious nameless and faceless fugitive as solitary as he.

Night. The last familiar noises from the Mahanaim camps had abated. Nothing was moving on the other side of the stream, whose glittering waves were the only remaining signs that the world was world and still alive.

And the man, what was he doing? Was he on the lookout, scrutinizing the darkness out of which, at any moment, the event would spring? Jacob, son of Isaac, son of Abraham, was pondering, reviewing his situation. That was why he had chosen to leave the others and stay alone on this shore. He knew that his life was about to change. But not in what way. At this moment everything was still possible. One word, one move would suffice for Jacob to remain Jacob—and Israel a frightened old man's dream.

A self-examination that implies a questioning of his past. Early childhood memories, early quarrels with his older brother, early triumphs followed by remorse, early loves, early and late disappointments; so many events led up to the encounter he had just had with his uncle Laban and the one he would have tomorrow with his brother Esau.

Jacob was worried. Understandably so. Tomorrow he might die. His brother, whom he hadn't seen in twenty years, would not come to the appointment alone; he would be accompanied by at least four hundred armed men. What would tomorrow be made of? Jacob was afraid. He had been fortunate all his life; it could not go on indefinitely, not beyond this night. Tomorrow it would all be over. The debt would be paid. For every moment of happiness, for every gift of love received or given. Tomorrow Jacob would submit to Esau, his brother, his nemesis.

Tomorrow—but the night had just begun. Jacob should try to find a solution; there had to be a way out. What if he were to begin praying? What if he armed himself for the fight? Or then again, what if he offered his brother a new gift, even more beautiful than the others before? Nobody is insensitive to gifts . . .

In fact, had he the slightest understanding of practical

matters, Jacob would have tried to rest. He should have tried to unwind, sleep, take advantage of the few hours that were left. Tomorrow he would need all his energy, all his faculties. He should have taken care of himself. He did not. He could not, for this night would mark the beginning of a new adventure, the most important of all.

A strange adventure, mysterious from beginning to end, breathtakingly beautiful, intense to the point of making one doubt one's senses. Who has not been fascinated by it? Philosophers and poets, rabbis and storytellers, all have yearned to shed light on the enigmatic event that took place that night, a few steps from the river Jabbok. An episode told by the Bible with customary majestic sobriety. Do you remember?

. . . Jacob was left alone. And a man wrestled with him until the break of dawn. It was a silent struggle, silent and absurd. What did the stranger want? Nobody knew, not even Jacob. They wrestled until dawn, neither uttering a word. Only then did the assailant speak: *Day is breaking, let me go.* And a suddenly belligerent Jacob refused, setting conditions: *I will not let you go, unless you bless me.* The other demurred; they clutched each other once more. Theirs was an awesome fight, yet in the end they had to give up, neither being able to claim victory. Both were wounded: Jacob at the hip, the angel in his vanity. Yet they parted friends, or was it accomplices? Jacob accepted his aggressor's departure willingly; the latter, as if to thank

him, made him a gift: a new name which in generations to come would symbolize eternal struggle and endurance, in more than one land, during more than one night.

This unknown, oddly behaved aggressor, who was he? Who had sent him? And for what purpose? Was he even a human being? The Biblical text uses the word *ish,* man. The Midrash and the commentators elevate him to the rank of angel. As for Jacob—who should have known— he situated him higher yet: *I have seen God face to face, yet my life has been preserved.* The aggressor readily confirmed this appraisal: *Ki sarita im El*—Your name shall be Israel, for you fought God and you defeated Him.

A confused and confusing episode in which the protagonists bear more than one name; in which words have more than one meaning and every question brings forth another. One constantly gets the feeling of being shut out, of watching an event through an almost opaque screen. What was it all about? Was the encounter accidental or deliberate? And this change of name—what exactly is a name? Is a man's self limited to a single name? And why did Jacob accept this new name? Did he not find his old one suitable?

We stumble on a secret even more impenetrable than that of the averted sacrifice of Isaac. There at least one felt that one understood, however superficially, why the characters acted as they did and what motivated them. Here we are left in total darkness. We understand neither the aggressor nor the victim, nor even the circumstances of their meeting. They seem to have spoken without communicating. The questions did not correspond to the answers. The words, the blows, the compliments—all seem irrational. The whole incident appears almost parenthetical, though clearly not without meaning.

To better comprehend the aggressor, let us examine his victim, Jacob. He is, after all, well known, more so than his parents and grandparents. From the moment of his birth, and even earlier, his every deed—and misdeed—was officially recorded. His reluctance to come into this world, clinging as he did to his twin brother's ankle. His extreme shyness. His education, his adolescence, his differences with his blind old father, who favored his older brother. His flight to Laban, his romantic adventures. We know that his mother protected him, perhaps a little too overtly. And that his children caused him concern: they hated their own brother Joseph, forcing him to become an expatriate in order to build himself a career.

Two events marked Jacob's life; three left an imprint on his legend: a dream about a ladder he did not climb, a gift he received without having solicited it, a secret he desperately tried to reveal without success.

The gift, as we saw earlier, was that of a name.

Let us reread the passage in the Bible: . . . *Jacob was left alone. And a man wrestled with him until the break of dawn. When he saw that he had not prevailed against him,*

*he wrenched Jacob's hip at its socket. He said: Let me go,
for dawn is breaking. — Jacob answered: I will not let you
go unless you bless me. — And he said: What is your name?
— Jacob answered: Jacob. — Whereupon the other said:
Your name shall no longer be Jacob, but Israel, for you
have wrestled with God and have prevailed. — Jacob then
asked: Pray tell me your name. — And he answered: Why
do you wish to know? And he blessed him. — Jacob named
the site Peniel: For I have seen God face to face, yet my life
has been preserved.*

It is almost like a mystical poem, barely coherent,
barely intelligible, not only to the reader but even to the
protagonists. Why did the nocturnal visitor attack poor
Jacob whose very name he claimed not to know? Because
he was Jewish? Or because he was alone and far from any
inhabited place? And why was the stranger so intent on
learning the identity of his victim? If he didn't know it,
why not have inquired before assaulting him? And if he
did know it, why did he ask? And why would he not
disclose his own identity to Jacob? Of the two, Jacob was
the "Jew," yet it was the stranger who answered questions
with questions. Until he ran out of them and then he
changed the subject—and Jacob let him! And why did
Jacob hold him back when logically he should have
shouted with joy that finally he was rid of him? And how
did the nocturnal visitor, with the advent of dawn, turn
into . . . God, in the eyes of Jacob?

This is one of the most enigmatic episodes in Jacob's life

and even in Scripture. One that ended well for him, since it brought him a new dimension—secret and sacred—a dimension he seemed to need.

For indeed, of the three patriarchs, Jacob is the least interesting. His life up to that point lacked greatness. There was nothing exceptional about his problems, his preoccupations. Abraham had been the pioneer, the conqueror, the founder of a dynasty; Isaac had been the survivor, the inspired poet. They both had the kind of charisma that Jacob evidently did not possess. Compared to his predecessors, Jacob seemed a personality of no real stature, with a mediocre, or at least commonplace, destiny. Without his adventure and metamorphosis at Peniel, he would have gone through history as a melodramatic and moving figure, but one lacking majesty and a sense of tragedy, a stranger to the events and conflicts of which legends and epic poems are made.

The portrait as drawn in the Bible—before Peniel—is striking in its pallor. It depicts a man straightforward but unimaginative, honest but anxious to avoid risks. An introverted, frustrated man, given to fits of temper, leading a marginal life. A weakling, manipulated by others. Everyone made him do things—and he obeyed. Such was his nature. Incapable of initiative, he could never make up his mind. His mother—Rebecca—gave him the idea of disguising himself as Esau, to deceive his father in order to exact blessings meant for another; she was the one who taught him the necessary gestures and answers. He cried but he obeyed. And it was Rebecca who, once the act was played, advised him to go away for a while, to take refuge with his uncle Laban, and again it was she who gave him his instructions for the journey, including whom not to marry. Naturally, he promptly fell in love with the first girl he met—Rachel—and blushing like a shy adolescent, wanted to marry her on the spot. Yet somehow he ended up marrying her sister. Doubly unhappy, he loved someone he could not marry and was loved by someone he had married without love. He did not complain about it, not too much, anyway.

He accepted life as it came, preferring to follow rather than be followed. Some seven years later, after he had married Rachel too and was blissfully living with the two sisters and two women servants as well, he would let them decide amongst themselves which one would spend the night with him. When Rachel took away her father's images and idols, she did not find it necessary to inform him. No one ever did. Both innocent and guileless, he took only what was handed to him. The only time he showed any independence was when he glimpsed Rachel for the first time at the edge of the well. He walked up to her and kissed her immediately. Yet the next moment he burst into sobs. Remorse? More likely, he was startled by his own audacity. As a matter of fact, he seems to have cried quite often. As a child, as an adolescent, even as an adult he seemed forever on the verge of tears. He wept at home, he wept away from home. He kissed Laban and wept; he kissed Esau and wept. When others kissed him, they too wept. We get the impression of a big child yearning for love and protection. Nothing surprising about that; his possessive, dominating mother had obviously done her best to spoil him. She had been after him constantly: do this, do not do that; come here, do not go there. Of course, she had meant well; he was, after all, weaker than his brother, more gentle and frail; clearly in need of a buffer between himself and the world. And so she had covered him with affection to the point of stifling him.

The fact that Isaac was an outstanding personality did nothing to help. Isaac was taciturn, uncommunicative; he discouraged confidences and yet from beyond his silence one sensed the mystery of his youth. It was not easy for Jacob to grow up in the shadow of a man whom God had singled out and demanded in sacrifice. It was not easy for Jacob to be the son of the first survivor in Jewish history, the first witness of a holocaust.

Moreover, for reasons known only to himself, Isaac favored Esau. One wonders why. Father and son had nothing in common; in fact, they were complete opposites. Isaac was sickly and blind; Esau was strong and keen on sports, physically endowed for games and hunting. Isaac aspired only to serenity and meditation; Esau was attracted by blood and violence. Isaac spent his time at home; Esau was forever roaming the fields and forests. Isaac lived for things spiritual; Esau sold his birthright for a bowl of lentils. And yet the two understood each other perfectly. Isaac loved his oldest son, who eagerly returned his love. Was it because opposites really attract one another? Or perhaps because Isaac, true to his name, wished to push laughter to its outer limits, thus showing God that man too is capable of combining peace of mind with brutality? The fact remains that father and son were close. To the point where the following question becomes unavoidable: Aside from all legal considerations, what would have happened to the people of Israel if the decisive encounter had taken place between Isaac and Esau? Without Rebecca's intervention, without her intuition, her objectively immoral ruse, Isaac surely would have given his blessings not to Jacob but to Esau; then whose descendants would we be? What if Isaac had uncovered the stratagem? Are we then nothing but the result of a fortuitous encounter? Could Israel then not have been at all, or else been Esau?

Surely these doubts must have tormented Jacob. He must have felt vulnerable, on the defensive, ill-at-ease in his role, at fault with his father (to whom he had lied) and with his brother (whom he had cheated) and with the entire world for which he was playing out a role. He had deceived others too often, he now thought of nothing but penance, of suffering to expiate his fault and redeem himself. That was why he submitted quietly; that was why he often wept without uttering a word.

People were exploiting him? Never mind! They were cheating him? Never mind! They were using him against himself? Never mind! The more they hurt him, the more reassured he seemed. When the blows became too hard, he took refuge in dreams, thus becoming the first dreamer in Biblical history. Abraham had visions, Jacob had dreams. When one dreams, the world and its laws seem better.

When Jacob dreamed, he transcended himself and became sublimated. His dreams transformed him—taught him that life is a ladder and that ladders lead up . . . and down. Nobody ever remains in one place, no suffering lasts indefinitely, every error may be corrected, perhaps erased. These were easy dreams, dreams of consolation. Neither demanding nor severe, God showed him His charitable side: *Do not be afraid, Jacob, I shall remain with you.* The very words that Jacob needed. More than Isaac, more than Abraham, Jacob had a constant need for personal reassurance and outside approval. Even when he heard what he wanted to hear, he could not believe in his mission. His very covenant with God became conditional: *If You will give me bread to nourish me and clothes to wear,* then I shall say yes and go wherever You will send me.

Here again: What was he asking for? Food, clothing, security. How disappointing. Jacob's dreams, while not lacking in grandeur and scope, were clearly neither metaphysical nor mystical. He lacked imagination: whatever he did, whatever he said, whatever he asked for was commonplace. To the point where one fails to understand why the Bible insists on overwhelming us with details: his quarrels with Laban, his labor contracts, his trivial conversations with wives and concubines. Was this what Jacob was all about? Nothing more? An insignificant dreamer who allowed himself to be taken in by the first comer, who fled from every contest, who gave up a fight without even trying? And this man who lacked both will and authority, this man who submitted to a search by Laban to prove that he had not stolen from him, could this have been the man chosen by God to plant the tree of Israel? Was there nothing left of Abraham's power, of Isaac's vision?

It is painful to say, but—before Peniel—we can claim no discovery, no triumph for Jacob; no heroic act has been attributed to him. Abraham and Isaac had been involved in extraordinary battles; their conflicts had touched the very core of man. Jacob? Concerned only with appearances, business matters, all manner of worldly endeavors; forever plunged in impossible situations, ready to be duped. Until Peniel no one ever heard him speak of anything other than the most down-to-earth matters, and even at Peniel he seemed far from having come into his own.

A Midrash: Upon awakening the morning after his first wedding, when he discovered Leah next to him instead of Rachel, he could not stifle a complaint: All night I was calling you Rachel and you answered me; why did you deceive me? And you, she retorted, your father called you Esau and you answered; why did you deceive him? And Leah even pushed her argument one step further: Is there a teacher without disciples?

Another text shows even greater contempt: When they saw how Jacob was overcome by fear prior to his encounter with his brother Esau, his women—all of them—asked sternly: Since you are so timorous, why did you make us leave our father's house?

Could this be Jacob, our ancestor? This man who did not even command respect in his own home, could he be the man who gave his name as a symbol to the most threatened, the most obstinate people in the world?

Usually—we said it before—the Midrash strives to balance the Biblical text. Jacob comes close to being the exception. Accounts of the period before Peniel are few and uninformative. Jacob failed to inspire the most outstanding and prolific storytellers in Jewish tradition: those of the Talmud. In truth, one understands them. What tale could possibly follow, that is, outshine, the adventure that had taken place at Mount Moriah? And so, instead of imagining legends that would seem pale in the shadow of the summit, they showered Jacob with pious compliments, they invented all sorts of virtues for him: he was charitable, pure, just, generous, radiant; his beauty equaled Adam's. They said that Abraham had been saved—retroactively—thanks to Jacob's intervention. Also: every generation has its Jacob, without whom it could not survive. And: he converted men to faith in God; he was righteous like Job and humble even though he never traveled without a retinue of less than sixty thousand guardian angels; he was studious, spending his time studying Torah at the academies of Shem and 'Ever, living there some thirteen years. And what did he do in his leisure hours? He recited Psalms, naturally. And so it goes: a few praises here and there, hardly enough to give stature to the character. Compared to his father, he can only lose. He does not even have an aura of tragedy. Of the two brothers, Esau seems the more tragic; he is the one who at a certain moment touches us most.

• • •

We feel sorry for him. From the beginning we are told that nobody loves him; the Bible is against him and the Midrash even more. The calumniations he is subjected to are surpassed only by those that were spread later about Israel.

His own mother seemed to resent him. She pushed him aside. Why didn't she love him? Because he preferred games to study? Because his hair was long and red? Because he always walked around armed? Because he was constantly hungry? She was hostile to him, that seems clear. And unjust.

And then, there was this younger brother who thought he was more clever than he and proved it by robbing him of his birthright. That too was unjust. And there was more: the plot contrived by his mother to allow Jacob to garner the blessings that Isaac had meant for him, was that just? And if all that were not enough, when Esau—cheated, robbed Esau—appeared weeping before his old father with a most humble request: to be blessed *as well* —one blessing, just one, was all he wanted—he was rejected. He did not ask his father to condemn Jacob, he did not demand justice; all he requested was one gesture, one word of tenderness, of consolation. And Isaac refused. The only person who had not conspired against him, who had loved him and wanted his happiness, now abandoned him too. Like the others. And that is when Esau uttered his terrible, desperate cry: *Father, have you but one bless-*

ing to give? Is all lost forever? Are you repudiating me too, Father? Shall I remain friendless in this life which I endure and which endures me without joy or hope? But Isaac refused to be moved. Too late, he seems to have said, what has been given cannot be taken back; one may not go back on one's word, no matter how wrong one may have been. Isaac had planned to make his eldest son into a master; now he would be a slave. As a result of a hoax? Yes, as a result of a hoax. *You shall live by the sword!* said he to his son. Was it advice? Or a premonition? Was he suggesting that in the future he had better defend his rights and interests by force? In any event, it was not a blessing—not for Esau, nor for anyone else.

And yet. Years later, when the two brothers met again —after Peniel—Esau forgot the iniquities and scandals he had suffered and showed himself magnanimous and human; he kissed his brother and wept.

Admittedly, the scene has style. But it is Esau who emerges to better advantage. The Midrash sensed this and tried its best to see that Esau remained the villain. Thus we are told—quite seriously—that when Esau kissed Jacob he meant, in fact, to bite his neck. Only, miraculously, his neck turned to marble; and that, of course, was why he began to weep—in rage and pain. Also: Jacob was protected by invisible angels who prevented Esau from harming him; that was why Esau did not take revenge— he was afraid. In general, he is described as a deceitful, evil and cruel human being. And a hypocrite to boot. We are warned not to trust his beautiful rhetoric or his expressions of charity. Just as Jacob came to symbolize the spirit, Esau came to represent instinct.

Yet in the Biblical text it is Esau, after all, who comes out better. He is described as strong but kind, wounded but tolerant. Not one to hold a grudge. Never mean. Better yet: truthful. More so than his young brother, who deceived him again: *I shall visit your home, at Mount Seir,* Jacob promised. Nowhere is it recorded that he kept his word or even that he meant to. He simply wanted to get rid of Esau as quickly as possible. And at any cost.

As for Esau, we marvel at his dignity and composure. He never wallowed in flatteries, as did Jacob. Jacob really did go too far; even his most vehement admirers concede that. He was wrong to speak of *expiation,* wrong to kneel seven times, wrong to address his brother as *Lord.* No man should humiliate himself before another, even his own brother and even if he is prompted by guilt or weakness. And no man has the right to reduce God to human scale when speaking of Him, just as no man has a right to attribute divine characteristics to man.

Why did Jacob humble himself before Esau? His self-punishment is all the more disconcerting because it took place *after* the struggle with the angel. We must deduce, then, that the struggle did not change him completely, after all. He was still incapable of breaking his bonds, of overcoming his fear. Something of Jacob must have remained in Israel.

• • •

He had been weakened by fear in the past. His most exalted dream, at Beth-El, had almost ended in disaster. Let us listen to the Midrash:

It is written that Jacob, in his sleep, saw a ladder that reached from earth into heaven and angels were going up and down.

Which teaches us that the Almighty, blessed-be-His-name, showed our father Jacob:

The king of Babylon going up and down,
and the king of Median going up and down,
and the king of Greece going up and down,
and the king of Rome going up and down.
And the Almighty, blessed-be-His-name, said unto him:
You too go up, Jacob!
But our father Jacob was afraid and answered:
They all have to come down,
and I might have to do the same.
And the Almighty, blessed-be-His-name, told him:
Do not be afraid, Israel,
if you go up now,
you shall never come down again.
But Jacob did not believe and hesitated,
unable to overcome his fear.
And then the Almighty, blessed-be-His-name, spoke thus:
Had you but trusted Me,
and gone up,
you would have remained up there,

all the way up there;
but since you failed to trust Me,
and did not go up,
your children, in exile,
will serve four kingdoms
and pay four kinds of levies
just like slaves.
And Jacob, seized by an even greater fear, cried out:
Will it last forever?
No, said the Almighty, blessed-be-His-name.
Not forever.

Reassured or not, the fact remains that Jacob could not free himself of either his anxiety or his weakness. He was gnawed by doubts and dared not integrate himself into this vision and obey the divine commandment: the future victor of Peniel trembled with fear at Beth-El.

Even the grandiose dream of the ladder, one of the high points of his life, is used by at least one commentator to illustrate his mediocrity:

On that particular night when the angels ascended into heaven they found there Jacob's image illuminated by divine splendor; it looked familiar to them. And so they hurried back down to admire the original. But they were disappointed and chagrined to find him . . . asleep.

Up there, in the universe of authentic and passionate dreams, Jacob was a hero, a prince who scorched others with his fire; but in his life on earth he was nothing but a tired old man who yearned only to sleep.

So then—and that is the question of questions—if Jacob was really this pallid, disappointing character who managed to sleep while God unveiled His plans for him, how could he become Israel?

At least we do know where to seek a possible answer. We know the place and we know the time: Peniel, on the night that preceded his encounter with Esau.

The metamorphosis could take place only at night. And in solitude. For Jacob represents human duality. His was a double life: during the day he discussed his affairs with his entourage; at night he spoke to God of immortality. We understand why. Crushed by Abraham's and Isaac's greatness, aware of his inferiority to them, Jacob viewed his own life as uninspiring, and suffered from that realization. The pioneers had tried it all, done it all; he could but follow in their footsteps. Distressed at not being able to also enter into the living legend of history, frustrated at having to deal with mundane and practical matters, Jacob found refuge in night. At night he was different. Transfigured.

At night he was his predecessors' equal; at night he lifted his gaze higher and saw farther; at night he too fills time and space and the tormented dreams of man.

Thus the decisive event of his life took place at night. At Peniel he was attacked, at Peniel he responded. Jacob, the nonviolent, the timorous, Jacob the weak, the resigned, the coward who always succeeded in avoiding confrontations, particularly violent ones, suddenly resisted the aggressor, plunged into the fight and returned blow for blow. And there was nobody around to come to his rescue, or even to give him moral support, or even to admire him. The metamorphosis seems so incredible, one wonders to whom or to what it should be attributed. To the attacker perhaps? Was he the one who succeeded in transforming Jacob into an inflexible and invincible warrior? Was this what Jacob had needed in order to become aware of his own strength, his own truth and the hopes he personified? Had he really needed an adversary, a dangerous adversary in order to become Israel? Does Israel owe that much to its enemy?

But who actually was this aggressor? The rabbinical accounts are not unanimous on the subject. The opinions vary greatly. He was a shepherd—no: a sorcerer—no: a sage—no: a bandit . . . The majority chooses to see him as an angel; besides, Jacob did not like to fight human adversaries. With an angel, well, that was different. But why would an angel attack him? For his own good, volunteers one text, to give him courage. After the struggle the angel was said to have told him: Look, I am a celestial creature and you defeated me, therefore you are wrong to fear Esau, you shall defeat him in no time at all.

The idea seems "logical" because it confers an immediate, almost practical meaning on the contest, even though it does reduce it to a training exercise.

Once the idea that it was an angel had been accepted, the Midrash tried to identify him. There are so many angels, each with his own duties and specific missions that one must take care not to confuse them. Said one sage: It was Esau's angel, the very one who in the higher spheres had been assigned to him—his good spirit, his inspiration and protector. Said another: Quite the contrary, it was Jacob's own angel.

I prefer this last hypothesis: Jacob attacked by his own guardian angel. The mysterious aggressor? The other half of Jacob's split self. The side of him that harbored doubts about his mission, his future, his *raison d'être;* the voice in him that said: I deserve nothing, I am less than nothing, I am unworthy of celestial blessing, unworthy of my ancestors as much as of my descendants, unworthy to transmit God's message to man.

Here the episode's dimensions shift: we witness a confrontation between Jacob and Jacob. Says the Midrash: God created the world so that day would be day and night would be night; then came Jacob and he changed day into night. Explanation: At Peniel, for the first time, Jacob behaved in the same way at night and during the day. That night the two Jacobs came together. The heroic dreamer and the inveterate fugitive, the unassuming man and the founder of a nation clashed at Peniel in a fierce and decisive battle. To kill or be killed. It was a turning point for Jacob. He had a choice: to die before dying, or to take hold of himself and fight. And win.

And win he did. Angel, other self or man, one thing is sure: the adversary was defeated. Now Jacob was ready to face his enemy brother. Or rather: he should have been. According to the Midrash, he was not. He continued to be afraid; worse, his fear now was twofold, one revealing text tells us. Jacob was afraid both of being killed and . . . of killing. He knew that one does not kill with impunity; whosoever kills man, kills God in man. And so he first had to convince himself that it would be possible to obtain a pure victory—pure of death, pure of guilt—a victory that would not imply the opponent's defeat or humiliation. A victory over himself. Such, then, is the prime meaning of this episode: Israel's history teaches us that man's true victory is the one he achieves over himself.

And yet it would be equally acceptable to give a more literal interpretation to the text and suggest that at Peniel, Jacob was forced into battle not with a human being or an angel, or even a self-image, but with Him who encompasses us all. Though almost unanimously rejected by Talmudic tradition, this hypothesis deserves close scrutiny. After all, Jacob himself lent it veracity: he himself never spoke of man or angel, or self-reflection. He spoke of God.

This may be meant to imply that there is a connection between divine and human solitude: man must be alone to listen, to feel and even to fight God, for God engages only those who, paradoxically, are both threatened and protected by solitude. God, traditionally, elects to speak to His chosen in their sleep because that is when they are truly alone, removed from all alien presence to distract them.

But solitude contains its own share of danger precisely

because it inevitably leads to God; whoever meets Him is irrevocably condemned to another kind of solitude. Thus to be chosen signifies not privilege but dignity and responsibility. *And none shall see My face and remain living* means: None shall see My face and live as he did before. From his contest with God, Jacob emerged triumphant but limping; he was never to be the same again.

But then, was this not the secret desire that had tormented him for years: to break the shell, to burn his bridges and accomplish something real, something great, perhaps even unique?

Jacob had lived in ambiguity so long that he could no longer see clearly; he no longer knew the names of things and beings, hence the accent placed on names by both adversaries. Jacob was no longer able to distinguish between Esau's protector and his own. From his earlier visions, he remembered what was expected of him: to project into history the people that would make history shudder. Was he capable of assuming the task? Was he worthy of it? He felt inadequate, incompetent; he wanted to understand himself fully. That was why he decided, on that particular night, to remain alone, this side of the river Jabbok. To rethink his life, to ask himself the questions one asks oneself before important encounters, encounters with the absolute—absolute good (God), or absolute evil (death, murder).

One can readily imagine his introspection, his self-examination: What have I done with my life so far? What have I done with the promises my father and grandfather received from God? I worked hard, I married, I had children, I became rich, I made enemies, I took detours, so many detours . . . I ran away, ran away so many times . . . I created nothing, accomplished nothing worthwhile, nothing authentic, nothing that transcends me, except in my dreams—but they were only dreams . . . Could this be the culmination of the history fashioned by Abraham and Isaac? Could Abraham and Isaac have gone to Mount Moriah only to produce this lackluster destiny that is mine? Compared to their adventures, his seemed drab and gray to him; devoid of all tension or even interest. God had played an active part in their experiences, not in his. In his own experiences Jacob competed with nothing but merchants, property owners who pursued him for lowly, ordinary motives.

And why in fact was he, Jacob, always pursued, persecuted? Why he? At Peniel, Jacob could not help but wonder about this. Why was he, he in particular, the butt of every jealousy, every hate?

In his dream at Beth-El, God had shown him the Temple in Jerusalem, first in all its splendor and then in ruins, with his descendants dispersed among the nations, hounded, massacred. Now, during this night at Peniel, he must have asked himself the awesome question: How are the victims responsible for the evil inflicted on them—to what extent are they to blame for arousing rancor and hate in their enemies—or in their neighbors turned enemies?

On this night, before the final battle with his brother—who could have been here in his stead—Jacob wanted to commune with himself, do something with his solitude, provoke a change—a mutation?—in his existence. And thus prove himself worthy of his parents.

Peniel: crossroad, dramatic turning point in Jacob's mind. No longer was he content to be the son of Isaac and the grandson of Abraham; he yearned to have a name all his own, fraught with a significance all his own and linked to an event that would immortalize him or destroy him— no matter, as long as it was as great, awe-inspiring and transcendant as the sacrifice there at Mount Moriah. So obsessed was Jacob by the story of that ordeal that he ached for an ordeal of his own. No more petty bargaining for him, no more conversations about trivia, no more family games. Jacob was determined to surprise others— and himself. Like his father and grandfather, he wanted to engage God in dialogue, no matter how great the risk. It was God he wished to confront. Not in a dream, but standing erect and with his eyes wide open.

The adventure at Peniel? A conscious, deliberate act, a challenge by Jacob. The battle? Conceived and arranged by Jacob. The initiative was his, so was the stage setting. Laban had already left and Esau had not yet arrived. What better moment to show Abraham and Isaac that he was lonelier than they ever were, that he was capable of going further than they ever did? They had submitted to God, but the idea had come from God, whereas he, Jacob, had provoked this confrontation. It was a challenge without precedent. He had not endured the harrowing experiences that marked his father nor had he accomplished the extraordinary feats of his grandfather, but he would show them that he too had the stuff pioneers are made of; no man before him had revealed to other men the battle God wages against them; no man before him had compelled God into open contest with man; and no man before him had ever established relations of provocation with God.

That night, at Peniel, Jacob suddenly discovered another self. A more perceptive, freer self. And never did he command so much respect.

Who was Jacob? The son of a survivor. And as such, it was difficult for him to live in his father's house. Isaac never spoke of the past. Yet Jacob wanted to know, to understand, for he loved his father. Still, in a curious way, he envied him. He was jealous of his grief, his memories. Jacob knew that no event would ever surpass the one that had taken place on Mount Moriah, and that troubled him. And so he tried to live dangerously, in his own way. He quarreled with his parents, argued with his brother, seemingly thriving on this existence filled with the blows and stumbling blocks of his own making. Threatened from all sides, he made a show of impassiveness in the face of adversity that reminds one of Isaac on the altar. Traveling from country to country, from refuge to refuge, as Abraham had done before him but for different reasons, Jacob left behind him a trail of resentments and jealousies. He seemed pleased when he was hunted. But deep down he knew that it was not the same, that it would never be the same. An enemy brother cannot be likened to an enemy father. Mahanaim was not Moriah, just as a ghetto in New York or Detroit is not, and cannot even be compared to, the Warsaw ghetto. Next to his father's life, his own seemed flat and bland. He was born too late, after the event. Was there anything left for him to hope for, to cry over? He had not even suffered. He could never know the agony of a man helpless between a father and his God, one as demanding as the other, in a world made of indifference. Moriah to him was a mountain like any other.

This is the context in which we must reread the episode at Peniel. Jacob needed to provoke God to justify his place in history. Only thus could he surpass himself and become Israel.

And as dawn broke, he did become Israel. He had to cross night, go to the end of the confrontation—face solitude and anguish—to become worthy of his name.

At dawn Jacob was a different man. Whatever he touched caught fire. His words acquired a new resonance; he now expressed himself as would a visionary, a poet. Jacob's strength is named Israel, says the Midrash. Did he win the battle? Can man defeat his Creator? Obviously that is impossible; but is it not a privilege to be defeated by God?

The Midrash, always cautious, stresses the angelic nature of the assailant. Though powerless before God, man is capable of defeating the angels.

Let us listen to another story:

When the battle was over, the angel pleaded with Jacob

to let him go; Jacob refused to leave without a blessing.

— I cannot, said the angel. I do not have time. Dawn is breaking and I must leave.

— You are afraid of dawn? Why? Are you perhaps a thief? Or a nocturnal gambler?

— No, but I am expected in heaven to sing the praises of the Almighty.

— You have friends up there, said Jacob, unperturbed. Let them sing.

— They will sing without me today. But that means that I shall never again sing with them. Tomorrow they will tell me: You didn't come yesterday, you are no longer one of us.

— You talk too much, said Jacob. The angels who visited Abraham blessed him before they took their leave. Do as they did.

— Impossible. It's not the same at all. They came for that purpose. I did not.

— Then you are not leaving.

Faced with Jacob's stubborn insistence, the angel changed the subject and began to speak not of blessings but of divine mysteries. Said he:

— The angels who revealed God's mysteries were exiled for one hundred and thirty-eight years—would you wish me to share their fate?

Jacob could have replied that the condition he had set was not related in any way to theosophy, but he was in no mood to argue:

— Either you bless me or I shall not let you go.

— So be it, said the angel, resigned. I shall reveal to you that which should not be revealed. And if God asks me why, I shall answer that a prophet's injunction takes precedence over *all* others.

Israel is decidedly no longer the sentimental and disoriented Jacob we have known until now. He has learned to be tough and resolute. To defeat his foes and command the respect of the angels. Oh yes, he could contemplate Peniel and remember it with pride.

And yet. A few short hours later he was trembling again as he faced Esau. His old fear come back? His old guilt feelings? That would have been only human. His victory over the angel had not solved his problems with man. Human problems can be resolved only on a human level. Angels might conceivably want to give in to man, but man does not. As far as Esau was concerned, Jacob continued to be Jacob and not Israel.

But there is something else. In the beginning the text speaks of man first and then of God so as to underline Jacob's progress. Jacob has just understood a fundamental truth: God is in man, even in suffering, even in misfortune, even in evil. God is everywhere. In every being, not only in the victim. God does not wait for man at the end of the road, the termination of exile; he accompanies him there. More than that: He is the road, He is the exile. God holds both ends of the rope, He is present in every extremity, He is every limit. He is part of Jacob as He is part of Esau.

And when Jacob knelt before Esau, it was not only to plead for mercy but also to discern and recognize God's will in Esau's. But there he went too far. To acknowledge that an enemy is carrying out God's will is one thing, to humble oneself before an enemy is another. God may be the enemy, but the enemy is not God.

Jacob won his share of eternity, but he emerged a shaken, shattered man. Jacob or Israel? Both. True, God ordered him not to call himself Jacob any more, yet one moment later the Bible calls him just that. As though Israel did not succeed in severing his link to Jacob. We are explicitly forbidden to call Abraham by his former name, Avram, but such is not the case for Jacob. For with him, we are dealing with the very destiny of Israel—the immanent, real, historical people of Israel as well as the eternal, meta-historical Israel. Could Israel have erased Jacob? No, he *should* not have—even if heaven had ordered him to do so. Israel would not have been Israel had he not first been Jacob, had he not carried inside himself Jacob's strange and exalted dream.

Tormented, torn, staggering under the weight of his memories, Jacob belonged to Israel just as Israel was part of Jacob. More than his father and his grandfather, Jacob was conscious of the pluralism that was to mark his descendants. Contrary to his father's and his grandfather's children, his children all entered Jewish history, even the exiled ones, even the Ten Lost Tribes. Jacob is the entire house of Jacob, Israel is the entire community of Israel.

Hence his obsession, in his old age, with the problem of exile. In his dreams he had seen the Temple go up in flames over and over again. Before dying, he would have liked to know when it would all end.

As he lay on his deathbed he summoned his children to gather around him so as to disclose to them the ultimate mystery of redemption—the end of time, the end of history. Here, again, he went further than either his father or his father's father. God allowed him to see further than his predecessors, and further than his successors, all except Daniel. But, says the Midrash, at the moment he was about to translate his vision into words, his prophetic gifts were withdrawn.

That was the most poignant, heartbreaking moment of his life. He had entered the most secret of sanctuaries, he had beheld the most luminous of beings, and now he passionately yearned to transmit, to teach, to make known what he had seen—and he could not. He could but look. In silence.

Listen to a Midrash: Jacob was about to open his mouth when he was beset by doubts: surely his insight was limited to Israel's destiny. How was he to know whether his descendants would remain in Israel's fold? He was wrong to doubt; for that doubt cost him his powers. In other words: the story he did *not* tell is more beautiful than the others—all the others—those told in his name and even those told by himself.

And yet, his intuition was right. He anticipated how

difficult it would be for Israel to remain Israel, and how much suffering, how many ordeals were in store for the sons of Israel. How could he not at least attempt to console his children? To urge them not to lose hope? To tell them that every exile has its boundaries just as every night meets the dawn? He had to tell them something—only the words ceased to obey him. And so, all that was left for him to do was to bless his children. Did he recall Peniel? The angel, the blessing, the victory? He died taking along his secret, the secret named Israel, this first ray of dawn to separate night and its specters from day and its pitfalls.

Yes, we know the place, we repeat the story—over and over. Somewhere in the valley the last shadows withdraw, rending the night and the silence. Dawn is breaking.

For the second time a man crosses the river Jabbok, listening to its murmur. He seems calm, calmer than before, yet tense. What if all this was only a dream? He seems melancholy but determined. He may have to fight. And kill. And die.

But he is no longer alone.

PARABLES AND
SAYINGS IV

I*t was to protect Jacob that his mother Rebecca sent him
to her brother Laban.*

*She knew Esau: capable of anything, the worst. Better
that Jacob go away, hide. Else Esau will kill him and—
thought the mother—*I will lose two sons at the same time.

*Question: Assuming her fear was justified and Esau
killed Jacob, would she not in fact have lost only one son,
not two?*

*Answer: Were Esau to kill Jacob, she would wish him
dead. For a mother, a murderous son is as dead as a son
who has been killed. If not more.*

*A Midrashic saying: Esau's strength and good fortune
and that of his descendants can be explained by the respect
Esau showed to his father.*

• • •

136

Another: Jacob and Esau both knew how to make others obey them. Jacob by his voice, Esau by his arm.

And this one: Like Abraham and Isaac, Jacob was chosen by God. But God did not draw him close. It was Jacob who, of his own volition, sought to come close to God.

Said Rebbe Menahem-Mendl of Kotzk: When Esau discovered that he had fallen victim to Jacob's deceit, he uttered a cry that seemed to come from the deepest recesses of his heart, and in front of his petrified father he shed three tears.

For these three tears Israel was to suffer the throes of exile. But, said the rebbe after a long sigh, there is a limit, there will have to be. Over the centuries we have shed so many tears, enough to make the oceans overflow, enough to flood the heavens. There is a limit, Lord, there must be a limit.

A Midrashic saying: Abraham is symbolized by a mountain, Isaac by a valley, Jacob by a house.

Why did Isaac's sight weaken? To enable Jacob, disguised as Esau, to come and gather the blessings.

• • •

In Jacob's vision of the future, he wept together with his persecuted descendants. And this was how he addressed God: In Your Book, it is written that one may not slaughter an animal and her young on the same day. This law shall not be observed by the enemy; he will kill mothers and their children in each other's presence. I shall not ask You who will observe Your Law; I shall simply ask You to tell me who will study it.

In his dream Jacob saw a ladder whose top reached into heaven. It still exists. There are those who have seen it, somewhere in Poland, at the side of an out-of-the-way railroad station. And an entire people was climbing, climbing toward the clouds on fire. Such was the nature of the dread our ancestor Jacob must have felt.

JOSEPH, OR THE EDUCATION OF A *TZADDIK*

THIS IS A STORY of dreams and dreamers. A frivolous, profane story. Seemingly concealing nothing in its depths, it brings into play every facet of human passion: love and hate, ambition and jealousy, glory and spite. Only one element is missing: the passion of God.

This Biblical tale is unlike any other. Expressed in terms of psychological intrigue or political conspiracy, there appears to be no metaphysical or theological dimension. God is not part of the cast. As if to illustrate that in a situation where brothers become enemies, God refuses to participate and becomes spectator.

A strange story it is, filled with spectacular turns of fortune, accompanied by shouts, tears and fury. Its heroes are warriors and prisoners, beggars and princes who know but do not recognize one another: characters in search of a destiny.

Beautiful and disquieting, it is also a tale about love—

139

sublime love, lost and cursed love; it fairly bursts with tensions, quarrels, silence and . . . waiting, waiting most of all.

In my hometown, when I was a child, this story was performed on Purim. Perhaps to mock Ahasuerus, the pagan king who fell in love with a beautiful young Jewish girl, we juxtaposed his story to that of the Jewish prince passionately loved and pursued by a heathen woman. Joseph made us laugh and cry, made us feel sad and proud: it is easier for a woman, if she is beautiful, to become queen than for a Jew to become prince. That is what this story is all about: man's capacity for transformation. The tale of Joseph is the tale of a metamorphosis—no, a series of metamorphoses.

First, a family metamorphosis: a favorite child falls victim to his own prerogatives. A social one: a poor immigrant becomes a huge success in his adopted country. A political one: a servant turns activist and changes the socio-economic policy of the land. A philosophical or artistic one: the slave turns into a prince. And finally, a purely Jewish metamorphosis: a young refugee, without friends or connections, builds himself an astounding political career culminating with his accession to the post of chief royal advisor.

No wonder that in our traditional literature Joseph is the object of passionate admiration bordering on worship. Here is a Jew whose tribulations had a happy ending, who owed his success to no one, who imposed his ideas on hostile surroundings thanks only to his natural gifts, who transformed exile into a kingdom, misery into splendor, and even humiliation into mercy. He was indebted to no one and that made him a free man, a man free to do whatever he chose.

For the Midrashic storytellers, his life is a veritable gold mine. Joseph: a feast for the imagination. There existed no Jewish nation as yet, but there already was a Jewish prince, a Jewish viceroy—how could one not applaud, not celebrate? He was loved because he illustrated the fact that for Israel the impossible is possible, and that in him and through him the Jewish child proved stronger than his enemies, stronger even than his temptations. In him the Jewish child lived and grew without betraying himself or his childhood. One loves him more, and more readily, more joyously than any other Biblical figure. Abraham is respected and admired; Isaac is pitied; Jacob is followed; but only Joseph is loved. Joseph: the sublimation of the Jewish child.

Talmudic imagination has turned him into a sort of superstar. His very name is said to have caused the angels to tremble. We owe him the miraculous crossing of the Red Sea. But also, said an ancient sage, all the sufferings to be endured by Israel until the end of time are rooted in those inflicted on Joseph by his brothers. In the Zohar, his mystery is linked to the mystery of Moses; in fact, his is the greater of the two. Among the ancestors, no other had a right to his surname: *Tzaddik*. Abraham was obedient,

Isaac was brave, Jacob was faithful. Only Joseph was just.

Just—he? He who married a woman who was not Jewish, a daughter of Egypt who brought up his children among pagans? He who led a life of luxury in the splendor of the royal palace? He who wielded quasi-absolute power and seemed to love it? What did he do to deserve this prestigious title?

True, he did send for his old father rather than settling him into an old-age home; true, he was not ashamed to show himself in public with his poverty-stricken family. But were those sufficient reasons to hold him up as an example, to proclaim him *Tzaddik?*

To gain a better understanding, let us try to sketch his portrait. And see whether behind the façade, the man is really what he appears to be, and whether, after all, it does not conceal an intense and complex inner life.

Joseph, the just and kindly prince, wise and competent, sure of himself and domineering. What was he really like? Let us first consult the biographical data contained in the Bible, where he occupies a major place: four weekly portions—or *Sidroth*—deal exclusively with him. Of all of Jacob's children, he is the only one who is treated as an individual, with a distinct destiny of his own. His life is narrated with a wealth of details: the circumstances surrounding his birth, the nature of his relationships with his father and his brothers, his adventures in the desert and later in Egypt. We are told how his brothers sold him when he was seventeen and how he became prince of Egypt at thirty, and finally, how he died at a hundred and ten. Nothing is held back: his failures and his triumphs, his moods, his habits, his talents, his friendships, his dreams, his political exploits, his amorous conquests. Nothing is left out, not only in the Midrashic tales, where one is used to it, but even in Scripture, where the literary flaws of the text are surprising. The narrative is too long, too slow, too transparent, it lacks both mystery and momentum. Compared with the chapters dealing with the sacrifice of Isaac or Jacob's encounter with the angel, it seems overwritten and overstated, each episode is retold three times, reiterating obvious points. It all seems clear and simple. Too simple.

And also, not only is the cast too large, its characters all run off in different directions. We have difficulty focusing our attention on any one protagonist, any one crisis, any one conflict. So much dispersion is disconcerting. Abraham's problem was his confrontation with God; Isaac's his confrontation with his father; Jacob's, his confrontation with his brother. But Joseph's? He has too many problems, involving so many people that the reader is at a loss as to which clue, which thread to follow to untangle the plot. To begin with, what is the major theme? The father's sadness? The brothers' malice? The Pharaoh's candor? The yearnings of a frustrated wife? The intrigues at the royal court? The Aristotelian rules of theater are violated; there is no unity of time, place or action. What we have is an incredible epic, unfocused, panoramic, disdainful of detail and lacking the terseness and sobriety of a work of art.

At first glance this seems to be also true of the principal character: his was a political awareness, not a poetic one. Shrewd rather than wise, he was a manipulator rather than a witness. Superficially melodramatic rather than genuinely tragic. He charmed people; made them weep but never meditate. His career? A series of disasters and successes, all fortuitous. It is all black or white, with nothing in between. We are told when he won and when he lost, and why. We see him isolated or surrounded, happy or distraught. We see him too much.

And yet he stirs our imagination. After all, he was the first Jew to bridge two nations, two histories; the first to link Israel to the world. He was no ordinary figure. Everything happened to him, and never on a petty scale. In defeat, he touched the bottom of the abyss. In his glory, he was the peer of kings who regarded themselves as peers of the gods. He was anything but mediocre, anything but boring. He conceived project after project and made them all come true. The Bible describes him as a "successful man." He knew how to impose his will on others. He aroused hate or love, fear or admiration. Never indifference. Some sought him out, while others avoided him, but nobody failed to notice him. Nobody failed to take a stand for or against him. He was to be found everywhere, embroiled more often than not in incredibly complex situations which he usually enjoyed confusing even further. While still a child, he behaved like a king. When he became king he often behaved like a child. His self-confidence was boundless; he loved to shock people and knew he could do so with impunity.

He was also an actor. Whatever he did, he did—or performed— in public. The most intimate of his dreams, he felt compelled to disclose. He saw himself as being constantly on public view, onstage, playing the most unexpected roles. He needed his audience.

In the context of the Biblical narrative, he was a new kind of hero, heralding a new era. Gone were the heroic days when God was present at every phase of the human adventure, influencing in direct or subtle ways the decisions of His chosen. Joseph: the emergence of a new style. Joseph: Israel's first link with secular history. Joseph: one family's flight, one nation's exodus—the tumultuous beginnings of a mission carried through the centuries. Joseph: the spoiled child.

His father loved him and forgave him everything because he reminded him of his dead wife, the beloved Rachel. The Midrash adds that he also resembled his father, or more precisely, that they followed similar paths, encountered similar obstacles and resorted to similar means to surmount them. Both were hated by their brothers, both ran away to live—and die—in exile.

But unlike Jacob, Joseph was his father's favorite son. Jacob refused him nothing. He owned the most beautiful clothes, for he liked to be regarded as graceful and elegant.

He craved attention. He knew he was the favorite and often boasted of it. Moreover, he was given to whims and frequently was impertinent. Arrogant, vain, insensitive to other people's feelings, he said freely whatever was on his mind. We know the consequences: he was hated, mistreated and finally sold by his brothers, who in truth were ready to kill him.

When he arrived in Egypt he quickly demonstrated his extraordinary skills. First as "psychoanalyst," then as "manager," statesman, counselor and the king's right-hand man. He was an extraordinarily inventive organizer, a forerunner of long-term government planners. With a difference: luck was on his side, his plans did not fail. In fact, he succeeded in whatever he undertook. Moreover, his predictions had a way of coming true. Also, he was handsome, affable, a ladies' man; he attracted them and they, in turn, attracted trouble. Never mind, he could handle such problems. He even succeeded in resisting temptation, winning on every score. He had the best of this world and clearly was destined to do as well in the next; he was not a *Tzaddik* for nothing.

Viewed as an entity, his life is a perfect illustration of Kierkegaard's concept of man's existence as divided into four cycles: the first being that of beauty, the second that of morality, the third that of laughter, and the fourth devoted to things sacred.

As an adolescent, Joseph was concerned only with external appearance and behavior. Later, in prison, he discovered the phenomena of good and evil. Still later, when he was king, he ridiculed his brothers, laughing at their expense. And finally, toward the end of his life, his demeanor approached that of a saint.

Thus, there *was* some logic in his life. Between the adolescent's dream and its fulfillment, despite the speed and diversity of events, developments *did* follow a clear pattern. Joseph could not help but become king. And *Tzaddik.*

The Midrash, as usual, goes even further and suggests that he was just from the start, that he never ceased being just, not even in Egypt, not even in the private chambers of a lady who . . . well, anyway: he was handsome and she was not indifferent to his charms. Nor were other women. Says the Midrash: Whosoever saw him could not help but love him passionately, secretly. It goes on and on, devoting innumerable anecdotes to his romantic experiences.

The Biblical text itself is sufficiently graphic. Potiphar bought Joseph, who promptly turned his master's good wife's head. This Lady Chatterley of sorts fell madly in love with her young servant, who rejected her favors. She insisted, persisted. In vain. He ignored her advances, and then, one day when the house was empty, she collared him, used force. In desperation, Joseph ran away, leaving his clothes behind. Whereupon the lady pressed his garments against her bosom, stroking them and weeping, or so the Midrash tells us.

Well, it is always dangerous if not downright foolish to

say no to a beautiful woman, but especially if she is in love, and more so if she is wealthy and powerful: Joseph's next stop was prison.

On the surface, a commonplace episode, one that should have been ignored by the Talmud. Modesty between the sexes is supposed to be a Jewish virtue, so that logically the Talmud should have spared the reader. However, the opposite is true: the reader is treated to scene upon scene, with only slight variations, illustrating the ravages wreaked by Joseph in the hearts of Egyptian womanhood.

A story: One day a group of Egyptian high-society ladies gathered at the Potiphar residence. The lady of the house, in true hospitable fashion, served citrus fruits and set out knives to peel them. Suddenly in walked Joseph. And so moved and bedazzled were the ladies, they went into a state of shock . . . and cut their hands to the bone. This is what I must endure day after day, hour after hour, breathlessly moaned Madame Potiphar.

Was Joseph aware of his effect on the opposite sex? Probably. He dressed like a dandy, combed his hair according to the latest style and carefully developed a gait meant to attract attention. He obviously wished to please.

One does not provoke a woman unless one wants to. One does not love a woman—or a man—against one's will. Every relationship is a two-way affair. Joseph knew when to desist from his flirtatious and amorous maneuvers, Madame Potiphar did not; she was determined to seduce him. The Midrash tells us how: The garments she wore in the morning, she did not wear midday, and those she wore midday, she hung away come evening. And yet, in spite of this non-stop fashion show, Joseph resisted.

Did he really? Yes, that at least is sure. But from what moment on? Here opinions vary. Certain texts say: from the very beginning to the end he never knew temptation; a *Tzaddik* like him is above passion and lust. But then there are sources that admit to an awakening of desire on his part; they suggest that he may have let himself be carried away somewhat, perhaps even quite far, but that the *Tzaddik* in him intervened in time to save him.

Scripture says that Joseph had come to "carry out his duty" in the empty house. What duty? There are two versions. Rav says that the reference is to his customary domestic tasks. Shmuel is skeptical, he says no, the work in question was of a different, more private nature. One passage in the Midrash describes Joseph and Potiphar's wife in bed, naked. But then what happened? At the critical moment Joseph thought of his father and that brought him back to reality. He jumped out of bed and ran.

Another text claims that at first the beautiful and loving lady tried to discuss the matter, professing her readiness to do anything if only Joseph would give in. Here is part of their dialogue. Joseph: No, I cannot, I will not.—She: But why not?—He: I am afraid.—She: Afraid? Of what? —Joseph: Of your husband.—She: That's nothing to worry about. I'll simply kill him.—Joseph (in a cold sweat): No! What are you trying to do to me? Turn me not only into a rake but an assassin as well?

1 4 9

This rather bizarre and amusing scene obviously troubled our Midrashic narrators. It seems too unbelievable, one has the feeling the text must be incomplete, that somehow it conceals something unpleasant. Joseph could not have been as innocent as they would like us to believe. Or as virtuous. Let us listen to a conversation between a *matrona* and Rabbi Yossi. This sophisticated and witty woman was incredulous: How could a boy *bekol khomo,* in the midst of puberty, his blood afire, conceivably have surmounted his desire, his instincts, especially when faced with an experienced, passionate and stubborn woman such as Madame Potiphar? The *matrona* was too cognizant of human weakness not to have doubts. And Rabbi Yossi, embarrassed, found nothing better to fall back on than . . . faith, the irrefutable argument. He trusted in the veracity of Scripture. The Bible does not mislead us, he told the *matrona;* it conceals nothing, distorts nothing; it reveals all the misdeeds of all our greatest men. It tells of Yehuda's mistakes; why then would it lie about Joseph? If he had indeed succumbed to passion, the Torah would have said so.

One clue that should help establish Joseph's innocence is that he was thrown into prison. Had he said yes to the seductress, would she not have kept him at her side? Yet she and nobody else handed him over to his jailer, after first turning the facts around. Her reaction seems both feminine and human. To wish to please and fail: what worse humiliation could there be for a woman? When it

happened to her, Madame Potiphar took revenge by accusing Joseph of her own sins.

In all fairness, we ought to pose the problem the other
way round as well. What if, in spite of everything, *she* was
telling the truth? An unlikely hypothesis. It seems hard to
believe that Joseph, a slave and stateless, would have run
the risk of offending the mistress of the house, wife of his
owner and benefactor. It seems even harder to believe that
Madame Potiphar would have rejected him: he was handsome, attractive, irresistible, all legends attest to that. And
also, ultimate argument, who could believe for even one
minute that Joseph the *Tzaddik* could have uttered a lie?
A *Tzaddik* who lies? A contradiction in terms.

And that is how all the texts present him, as a *Tzaddik*.
Even later, when he was already ensconced in the royal
palace, success did not go to his head. He remained devout, bound to God and His commandments. One commentator insists that he observed the laws of Shabbat.
Another waxed indignant: Why only the laws of Shabbat?
What about the others? He observed them all, says another, and more! He was a *nazir,* an ascetic; he refrained
from drinking wine. We are told also that he was a . . .
hasid. Every Just Man, says the Talmud, has one charac-
teristic trait: his was devoutness. God-fearing, humble, he
whispered his prayers even while working. Moreover, he
had a superb command of the secular sciences; he mastered seventy languages . . . plus one: Hebrew. Naturally,
the Pharaoh took advantage of having such a talented

linguist at his court. Joseph was to teach him the sacred
tongue. And Joseph did try to guide him through an ac-
celerated course. It was a failure. Was it the fault of the
teacher or the pupil? The private lessons came to an end
—the only failure Joseph ever experienced in his long
career. All his undertakings, both in his private and public
life—including the rationing of food and the charting of
economic plans—were crowned with success. Yet he
never boasted. His modesty, it seems, was never at stake.

When he sent for his father, he told his brothers: Do tell
him of all the honors that have been bestowed upon me
here. What? wondered the great Rebbe Menahem-Mendl
of Kotzk. Such vanity on Joseph's lips? Did he really think
he could impress the pure, the saintly patriarch Jacob?
No, mused the rebbe, the message should be read differ-
ently: Do tell my father that I am capable of receiving
honors—and remain unaffected by them . . . Jacob had
nothing to fear; the wealthy and powerful prince was still
his son.

And Jacob let himself be convinced; he left his home
and settled in Egypt, reunited with his entire family at last.

But now let us pause once more to raise the obvious
question that has admittedly been troubling me: In what
way was Joseph a *Tzaddik,* a Just Man? What did he do
to deserve this rare distinction? Why is he considered a
Just Man, he and not Moses, for instance? Did he really

lead such a perfect, such an untainted and altruistic life? Was his behavior really so irreproachable, always?

Let us go back to his biography, and since it is so closely linked to the biographies of his father and brothers, let us take a closer look at those as well. One shocking fact becomes immediately evident: in this whole intricate narrative, not one of the characters behaved like a *Tzaddik*. None was entirely above reproach, none was truly engaging. Indeed, the whole family does not withstand scrutiny too well.

First, the brothers: quarrelsome, envious, resentful, constantly involved in sordid plots. Split into clans, they treated one another with contempt. The sons of Jacob's wives lived apart from the sons borne to him by his servants. Only Joseph had dealings with the latter. By the way, this did not prevent them from turning against him later; they joined the others when it came to throwing Joseph into the snake pit. In the matter of persecuting Joseph, they were all united. They should have felt sorry for their small orphaned brother, whose mother had died tragically; instead they pounced on him, harassed him. They should have tried to console him; instead they made him feel unwanted, an outsider. Their father favored him above all others, and why not? Jacob loved him best because he was unhappy. But they refused to understand and treated him as an intruder. He spoke to them but they did not answer, says the Midrash. They turned their backs on him. They ignored him, they denied him. To them he was a stranger to be driven away. How is one to explain their insensitivity? How can one understand their hate, their murderous scheming? Or the pain they inflicted on their father? Even if they wanted to punish Joseph, why did they torture their father?

Nor did they have much affection for one another. When the Egyptian ruler seized Shimon as a hostage, they did not go to his aid; they simply abandoned him. Later, when the same ruler tricked them by hiding a silver cup in Benjamin's bag and having them all arrested, they started the blows raining on the poor boy, accusing him of the theft. So the Midrash tells us. It also tells how, later yet, they turned against their leader, Yehuda. They excommunicated him, blaming him for not having dissuaded them from selling Joseph into slavery: Had you advised us to bring him home safely, we would have listened to you.

For it had been Yehuda's idea: better to live in bondage than die. A compromise the Midrash judges harshly: It is forbidden to praise Yehuda. When human life and dignity are at stake, one has no right to settle for half-measures; Yehuda should have fought to the end to save his brother, not only from death but also from shame.

The other brothers were worse. So jealous were they of Joseph that they wished to see him dead. When Joseph as viceroy staged the grand finale of the reunion and removed his mask, they were seized by a panic so great they tried —even then—to throw themselves on him and kill him.

Later, much later, after he had already forgiven them, they were still jealous. They accepted his gifts but kept their distance. They dared accuse their father of flattery because on his deathbed he dispensed more blessings to Joseph than to them. They grumbled: our father favors him and wants to please him because he is in power.

Understanding the father is just as difficult. Surely Jacob was the real culprit; he must have been a bad father, a poor teacher. What an idea to favor one child, give him more gifts, more attention, more love. Did he not realize how that was affecting the other children? That they felt frustrated and rejected? Did he not know that such behavior would eventually harm the boy he wanted to protect? Did he not see what was going on under his own roof? Did he ever try to reason with his older sons and thus bring peace into his home?

Also, and even more serious: it was Jacob himself who had sent Joseph to his brothers in Shechem. Just like that, on a visit. Had he no inkling of the dangers awaiting his young son? Why did he risk the boy's life or, at the very least, his safety? Did he not understand that his sons could hardly be expected to appreciate a visit from a brother who came at his leisure to watch them work? Could Jacob have been that blind?

And when his sons returned from Shechem and announced the terrible news to him: Joseph is no more; he has been devoured by a wild beast, Jacob believed them. He questioned them only superficially. He never went to investigate the site of the drama; he sought no confirmation, no corroboration! He accepted Joseph's bloodied shirt as irrefutable proof! Why didn't he try to elicit more details from Yehuda: how the tragedy had happened and when? And why did he not turn to God—he who never used to take a step without consulting Him—to obtain information if not intervention? There are only two possibilities; either Jacob was unaware of the hate his sons felt for Joseph—and then it is difficult to understand his blindness—or else he *did* know—and then one does not understand his passivity. What strange behavior for a father. Separated from his favorite son, he sank into a depression, was unconsolable, and yet he did nothing to find him or at least his mutilated remains.

Nor does one understand Joseph. He too eludes, and even disappoints, us. He seems not too appealing a human being, particularly in the beginning. First, his behavior toward his brothers left much to be desired. Instead of sharing his privileges, he flaunted them deliberately to arouse envy. A shocking lack of generosity for a future prince. Rather than bring his brothers closer to their father, he set himself up as obstacle. Parading in his expensive new clothes, he wanted to make certain that all the world see that while Jacob had many children, he, and he alone, was the chosen one, the superior one. He boasted about it so much and so often that he may have convinced himself. Small wonder, then, that he aroused such animosity. Even worse: he had a nasty tongue. He would mingle with the servants' sons only to bring back their gossip to his father. What sort of gossip? There are two versions. One: he told his father what people in the street and in the marketplaces were saying about his brothers; two: he told his father what the brothers themselves were whispering about Jacob. (And Jacob listened. Was that why he was punished? One Midrash suggests just that.)

We are allowed to see Joseph in action, playing one brother against the other, the father against all. He enjoyed dividing people, poisoning their minds, provoking tensions and quarrels. So total was his egocentricity that he apparently came to believe that all of creation existed only to serve him. Speaking of his success, the Midrash alludes to his character as that of a man who overturns all obstacles and breaks all resistance. Nothing and nobody could stop him; the universe belonged to him. And there were his dreams, revelatory as are all dreams. Jacob's dreams pertained to the universe, the Pharaoh's dreams to the Egyptian people collectively; Joseph's revolved around his own person, his own career.

Let us reread the Biblical text:

One day Joseph went to his brothers and said: Pray listen to the dream I have just had. We were gathering wheat in the field when suddenly my bundle stood up and remained standing while yours formed ranks and bowed to mine. To which his brothers answered, with understandable anger: What? You wish to reign over us? Unperturbed, Joseph told them another of his dreams: I saw the sun, the moon and eleven stars prostrate before me. This time it was too much; even Jacob took offense. Yet while Joseph had gone too far, Jacob still believed him, if only a little.

Listen to the Midrash:

Veaviv shamar et hadavar—The father took pen and

paper to write down his son's exact words as well as the date and place. One understands both the father's anger and his reluctance to dismiss the dream as fantasy. After all, Jacob knew about dreams, especially that it is safest to keep them to oneself. By blaming Joseph publicly, he may have hoped to attenuate the brothers' jealousy. But it is Joseph we really fail to understand. How could he, the future strategist, the born schemer, so shrewd and perspicacious, not know that certain dreams and certain dreamers inexorably spark opposition?

Above all, could this be the childhood, the education of a *Tzaddik?* This same question arises over and over again. When his brothers were getting ready to sell him, he began to plead for mercy, a Midrash tells us. Was that fitting behavior for a future *Tzaddik?* One expects a Just Man to accept all events, good or bad, serenely and perhaps even proudly. And what about the Potiphar affair? Surely it does not point to any overwhelming desire to lead an exemplary, austere life, a life aiming for purity and perfection. One does not get the impression that he came to the empty Potiphar residence with only his servant's tasks on his mind. Besides, if he was totally innocent in this affair, why did he not run away earlier? Why did he wait till the last moment?

And later, in prison, who were the people he befriended? The wretches of the earth? The eternally deprived? The dregs of society? Not Joseph. He became the intimate friend, the confidant of two former court officials. He even succeeded in getting himself appointed administrative director of the prison. Even in jail, he avoided misery and humiliation. Even in jail, he had to be first. Is that the path that leads to saintliness?

Let us continue. When he became viceroy of Egypt, he married an Egyptian: Osnat, daughter of the priest Potifera. True, the Talmud invented a bizarre story to explain that in reality she was not Egyptian at all but . . . Jewish; that she was in fact the daughter of Dinah, Joseph's sister, kidnapped at birth and left with Potifera. Of course, nobody was supposed to know this, not even Joseph, who did not realize that in marrying Osnat he was marrying his own niece. A convenient story, no doubt. But the fact that the Midrash felt compelled to invent it strongly indicates that misalliance there was.

According to all evidence, Joseph tried to adapt to his newly found country. One of his sons he named Menashe: *For God has made me forget all my tribulations and the house of my father.* And the other, Ephraim: *For God has made me bear fruit in the land of my misery.* The Midrash, as usual, goes further yet: When Jacob met his grandsons, he found them so alienated that he could not recognize himself in them. Is that the portrait of a *Tzaddik?* Jacob, says the Midrash, did not forget what he had studied— Joseph did. Joseph, the assimilated Jew.

Remember: during the long years of separation, Joseph, now a powerful prince, did nothing to obtain news of his father. Yet spying was common practice in those days and there were countless caravans. Why, then, did he let his elderly father, who had loved him so, despair and mourn for him? He was angry with his brothers, that we understand. But why did his father deserve such shabby treatment?

Later, when his brothers were brought before him, he sought only to ridicule them, to take his vengeance. Instead of inquiring about his father and his younger brother, he demanded hostages; instead of feeding them, he made them tremble with fear. Weeks and weeks went by before he deigned to reassure them. Ten times he heard his brothers refer to their father as *Your servant Jacob*, and unmoved, neither protested nor betrayed himself. Indeed, that cost him dearly. For every humiliating mention he did not acknowledge, he paid with one year of his life. He died at a hundred and ten, not at a hundred and twenty as had been planned. But forgetting the issue of crime and punishment, the question is whether a man so lacking in respect for his father's honor deserved the title of *Tzaddik* bestowed upon him by tradition.

Joseph had adopted Egyptian customs and tradition to the point that his brothers did not recognize him—which speaks in their favor rather than his. Luxury is more corrupting than poverty, happiness more corrosive than misery. In their eyes he was a foreigner, a man who had left his people, repudiated his roots; nothing remained of his childhood. No wonder they began by looking for him in the quarter reserved for prostitutes.

And yet. Joseph was and remains—in tradition and

legend—a *Tzaddik.* Why? By virtue of his deeds? Inevitably, we stumble on that question once more.

But let us try to turn it around and say that once raised, the very existence of the question lends Joseph a new density. Suddenly we suspect a secret. If, despite all that is said about him, he is *the* Just Man in the Bible, it must mean that we have been misled by appearances. We have been looking at a mask, we have not seen the face.

So far Joseph has impressed us as a sort of boastful, power-hungry politician. A second, more thorough analysis of his biography demonstrates our error. Joseph: the most misunderstood man in the Bible. More complex, more mysterious than one assumes at first. Through him, we are in touch with a tragic vision of Jewish fate, a vision worthy of his ancestors.

One recognizes the value of a text by the weight of its silence. Here the silence exists and it weighs heavily.

First, there is Joseph's astounding silence during the brutal scene at Shechem. All the brothers (except Benjamin) participated in it in one way or another. One imagines their discussions, one sees them hurling him into the snake pit. They wanted to kill him; they were about to kill him. And Joseph was silent. Face to face with his brothers, who shout their hate; face to face with the "sons of servants" whom he had befriended and who now have turned against him, like the others. Looking into their murderous eyes, he became mute. At the most critical moment of his life he let them deliberate, decide his fate, without uttering a word. Rabbinical tradition stresses that he began to weep, to plead for mercy only when his brothers prepared to sell him into bondage.

More striking still is Jacob's silence. From the day that Joseph was taken from him, he led a solitary, almost secret life. For twenty years he did not speak. Not a word, not a complaint. He lived outside language, beyond hope. Bathed in silence and penetrated by it, he was distant and inaccessible. He seemed to have cut his ties with the world and its Creator.

For, on another level, there was also the silence from above. God no longer spoke to Jacob and Jacob no longer addressed himself to God. The break was total.

The Midrash tries hard to explain God's silence. At Shechem, it says, the brothers took an oath of secrecy on the affair and also swore to excommunicate anyone who would break that oath. But every ceremony of excommunication requires the presence of ten people. Since the brothers were only nine, says the Midrash, they decided to make God the tenth. That was why God could no longer speak to Jacob; he had become an accomplice.

But Jacob's silence remains unexplained, inexplicable. He no longer seemed to pray, no longer seemed to think of God. Between God and him, there was only silence. During the entire period of uncertainty, those interminable years when Jacob needed to express his grief and hear a word of consolation, he said nothing. His relations with

God were renewed only after the family reunion. Only when Jacob hesitated to join Joseph in Egypt did God encourage him.

Suddenly we discover that during the entire narrative, the floods of words have but one purpose: to cover the silence. And that this silence in fact is the dominant theme. And also that the story is more beautiful than it appeared, and Joseph—the axis around whom everything revolves—more mysterious than he appeared.

The question that has been haunting us remains: In what way was Joseph the *Tzaddik* worthy of his title?

In the Midrash the answer is simple: because Joseph was able to overcome his sexual urges. Despite the atmosphere of overt sensuality that prevailed in Egypt, he resisted adulterous wives, Potiphar's and others: Day after day Joseph saw a number of princesses and courtesans, some covered with jewels, others with perfume, still others . . . with nothing at all; and every one of them was seductive. But Joseph remained chaste.

Another text offers this image: When Joseph went in and out of the royal palace, the princesses stood at their windows and threw him their jewels, earrings and bracelets, to attract his attention—but he never even looked up. For our ancient sages, that evidently was reason enough to crown him *Tzaddik.*

Not for me. I readily admit that a *Tzaddik* should be

able to resist temptations, but I would prefer to see the concept enlarged to include temptations beyond those inherent in sexuality.

First let us define the term *Tzaddik*. In Arabic it means friend. In Hebrew it is the opposite of *Rasha,* wicked. *Rasha* is he who sins against man, not necessarily against God. He who deserts his community is a *Rasha.* He who harms his friends is a *Rasha.* To betray one's comrades, to flout one's people, those are acts of a *Rasha.*

Conversely, the term *Tzaddik* is defined by relationships between men, not necessarily between man and God. A *Tzaddik* is he who resists temptations, not necessarily tests. Tests imply God; temptations are human. Abraham, tested by God, was not a *Tzaddik*. Joseph was.

Joseph had to overcome inner obstacles not in order to come closer to God, but to his fellow-men. His own brothers. He had good reasons to repudiate them, to hate them, to drive them from his house and memory; for him they represented a source of grief and evil.

He had equally good reasons to distrust women; the most beautiful and powerful among them caused him to be thrown into prison.

He had every reason to distrust people in general. He even had reasons to feel bitter toward his father.

Let us go back once more to the incident at Shechem. Joseph went there to meet his brothers, unaware that they were lying in ambush for him, ready to kill him. But who had sent him? Jacob. The visit had been his idea. He was the one who had asked Joseph to go and see his brothers, just like that, for no particular reason. At that crucial moment, while his brothers were binding him and throwing him to the ground, Joseph tried to understand, to remember. And suddenly a searing, terrifying thought crossed his mind: Was it possible that his father knew, and had sent him here because he *wanted* this to happen? Because he *wanted* him to be killed? The motive? Still the *Akeda*. The memory of Mount Moriah. At Peniel, Jacob had wanted to imitate Isaac; here he could be wishing to emulate Abraham by sacrificing a son, his favorite son.

Joseph, with his sharp, intuitive intelligence, could have reached a conclusion of this sort. Is it sheer coincidence that the two episodes, that of Shechem and that of Moriah, both open in fear and end with a miracle? And that both Isaac and Joseph are designated by the same word: *naar,* adolescent? And that, called by God, Abraham said: *Hineni,* here I am. While Joseph, sent by his father, responded also by *Hineni?* And that while Isaac was saved by the sudden appearance of a ram, Joseph was saved by a passing caravan? Does this explain why Joseph was so petrified that he could not speak? And why, hurt and humiliated, he decided later to break with his family and forget his past? How can one blame him? Did he not have valid reasons to repudiate his enemy brothers who had plotted his death? And to detach himself from their father, who had handed him over to them? And to opt against all of them and for the society that had offered him shelter and happiness? His hostile reaction was normal and human; had he not broken, or thought he had broken, definitively, completely, with his family's world and their laws? It was only natural that he felt closer to the Egyptians than to the Jews. And even to his political duties than to the God of the Jews. It was only normal that he withdrew from this family he could no longer love and thought of vengeance. Yet this was only a first impulse; he quickly pulled himself together: he would not be an avenger. There is rare virtue in forgoing justified reprisals, overcoming well-founded bitterness. It is not easy to resist dealing out deserved punishment. Only a *Tzaddik* forgives without forgetting.

Joseph forgave, but forgot nothing. In truth, he never forgot anything. He remembered his father at every moment and in every place. Though he could not understand some of his father's attitudes, he still thought of him. And he always remembered his people. At the height of his glory the Pharaoh gave him the surname of *Tzofnat Paneach,* the code-breaker, but he chose to keep his Jewish name: Joseph. Though he was worshipped, idolized by Egyptian nobility, he showed himself openly with his destitute family. Beneath a succession of masks, his loyalty had remained intact. He was on his way to the top, yet he knew when to halt, turn back and reassert his faith in his family in spite of them. And his faith in God, in spite of himself. That was his strength.

Any man who is fair-minded with one man or one group of men is fair-minded with all. By working for his people, a Jew helps mankind. Joseph was generous both with his kin and with his fellow citizens. He was the first to know how to reconcile his love for Israel with his love of other nations; he was the first to know how absurd and futile it is to oppose Judaism to universality.

A legend: Yehuda, the strongest of the brothers, confronted Joseph, whom he still believed to be an Egyptian potentate. The argument revolved around Benjamin. In his anger, Yehuda became capable of "crushing pellets of iron between his teeth." He shouted: If I unsheathe my sword, I shall destroy your kingdom from one end to the other. — Unsheathe your sword, and I will twist it around your neck, answered Joseph. — If I open my mouth, I shall swallow you, shouted Yehuda. — Open it and I shall close it with a stone . . . came Joseph's reply. Then Yehuda ordered his brothers to set the land on fire and lay it to waste. Only then, to save Egypt, did Joseph decide to stop his act; he dropped his mask: *It is I, Joseph, your brother.*

When he succeeded in vanquishing his bitterness and eventually transforming it into inspiration and love, he became a reconciled, happy man. At peace with his father, his brothers, his neighbors, his subjects. He reached his peak of achievement after Jacob's death. His brothers worried: As long as our father was alive, Joseph left us alone; now he will settle his accounts with us. To which Joseph replied: If ten candles did not succeed in extinguishing one lonely candle, how could one extinguish ten? Yes, he forgave, but he had forgotten nothing.

What does all this mean? That one is not born a *Tzad-*

1 6 7

dik; one must strive to become one. And having become a *Tzaddik,* one must strive to remain one.

There is in Joseph a duality which influences his deeds and his choices and makes him into a genuine, therefore torn, person. He lived on two levels, in two worlds, tossed back and forth by frequently contradictory forces. He had to choose and decide who he wanted to be. He had to choose to fight and win.

A tragic figure, Joseph is the father, or in any case, the forerunner of a Messiah, an unhappy, unlucky Messiah; the hero-victim who, according to tradition, must pave the way for the coming of the other, the true Messiah, son of David.

While the tribes were busy selling their brother, and Jacob was perfecting his fast, and Yehuda was taking a wife, God was busy creating the light of the Messiah, says the Midrash. A somber light, no doubt. For the Messiah it illuminated—Joseph's descendant—was to fall in combat heroically, tragically.

Joseph knew it, just as he knew or should have known that the kingdom of his descendants, the kingdom of Shilo, would be destroyed. And yet he did not give in to despair.

Joseph knew—and who was in a better position to know —that to be the first Jewish prince in history, to be the first to liberate Jews outside their homeland, would be difficult and unrewarding. A descendant of Yehuda's was to wear the crown of Jewish sovereignty, symbolizing eternal promise and eternal dawn.

168

And yet, Joseph did not despair.

He assumed his destiny and tried to give it meaning from within. He lived his eternal life in the here-and-now, demonstrating that it is possible for the slave to be prince, for the dreamer to link his past to the future, for the victor to open himself to the supreme passion that is love.

What a story: it tells us in one breath that the first exile was caused by the disruptive jealousy of men who were brothers; that exile leads to redemption if only one dreams of it without despair and . . . remains true to oneself.

Joseph was not born a *Tzaddik,* nor did he have the childhood or the education of a *Tzaddik;* that is why his triumph excites us. Whatever Joseph obtained from himself, he owed only to himself.

His reward? Moses personally took care of his funeral. Why such a privilege? Because while his ancestors had to deal with God and proved themselves worthy, Joseph had to deal with men and proved himself no less worthy. To suffer at the hands of God is less painful—or painful in a different way—than suffering the cruelty of men, even if they are our brothers, particularly if they are our brothers. Joseph, the first Jew to suffer at the hands of Jews, succeeded in mastering his grief and disappointment and linking his fate to theirs.

Joseph—a *Tzaddik?* The title was, unquestionably, deserved. In the Biblical text there is another adjective that describes him well: beautiful.

His only error: he should not have revealed his dreams.

PARABLES AND
SAYINGS V

J oseph had a sense for drama. To confuse his brothers, he told them that Joseph was alive and in his service. He called them liars and hypocrites for having told their father that a wild beast had devoured their brother Joseph.

Just you wait, I shall summon him and you will meet him. And he began to call: Joseph, Joseph, son of Jacob, come here, come here, son of Jacob. And all the brothers turned around, white with fear, scanning the four corners of the room for Joseph. Come here, Joseph, he went on, come and see your brothers who sold you. And the brothers looked and looked and didn't understand; there was nobody else in the room. Why are you searching in front of you and behind me? It is I, your brother Joseph.

Panic-stricken, they fainted. But God performed a miracle and brought them back to consciousness.

· · ·

The Talmud reproaches Joseph for having allowed those who spoke to him of his father to use the expression "your servant" ten times.

In the Bible, however, one finds the expression only five times.

Explanation: the conversation between Joseph and his brothers took place with the help of an interpreter who translated into Hebrew and Egyptian. And, of course, Joseph understood the two languages.

When God appeared to Jacob for the last time, He calmed his fears: I shall go with you to Egypt . . . Our ancient sages view this as a promise that the Shekhina—*the divine Presence—would follow Israel everywhere, even into exile; whence the certainty that even in exile Israel is never alone and that Israel's redemption will bring about God's as well.*

Saying from the Zohar: When Israel went into exile, so did its language.

Coming back from his father's funeral, Joseph made a detour and visited the site where long ago he had touched the bottom of the abyss; for a long time he stood at the well's edge and looked into the darkness. The brothers assumed that he did this to remind them of their misdeeds, but in truth he wanted to recall his past to himself so as better to express his gratitude to God; he was thankful for what he had been allowed to experience up to that moment.

The brothers told Joseph: Before he died, your father ordered you to forgive us. Yet in the Biblical text we find no mention of such a desire in Jacob.

Explanation: one may lie if it is on behalf of peace.

When Jacob's children settled in Egypt, they were at first prosperous, respected and content. Then people began to envy them secretly. Then openly. Still, that was not dangerous. But later, people began to fear them. To hate them. They were thought to be too rich. Too numerous. Pervasive, cumbersome. That still was not dangerous.

Came the time when the Egyptians found themselves embroiled in a bloody war with their neighbors. And owed their eventual salvation to the intervention of the children of Israel.

Only then did the danger that hung over the children of Israel become real. For that was something the Egyptians could not forgive.

And yet. As long as one child of Jacob was still alive, nobody dared attack the Jewish tribes. At the death of Levi,

172

the last living son, things changed abruptly. Soon appeared the first anti-Jewish measures: forced labor, public humiliations. Worse: laws were enacted forbidding the men to sleep in their homes, thus preventing them from loving and multiplying.

MOSES: PORTRAIT
OF A LEADER

A LEGEND:

When Moses went up to heaven to receive the Torah, he found God in the process of adding to it various symbols and ornaments. Conscious of his role as spokesman, Moses asked shyly:

— Why not give the Torah, such as it is? Isn't it rich enough in meaning, sufficiently obscure? Why complicate it further?

— I must, answered God. Many generations from now, there will live a man named Akiba, son of Joseph, who will seek and discover all kinds of interpretations in every word, in every syllable, in every letter of the Torah. So, you see, I must put them there, so that he may find them.

— Would you show me that man, asked Moses, impressed. I should like to know him.

Since there was nothing—or almost nothing—that he could refuse His loyal servant, God said to him:

— Turn around, go backward.

Moses did as he was told. He turned backward and found himself projected into the future. There he was, in a Talmudic academy, sitting in the very last row, among the beginners, listening to a master delivering a course on Moses' teachings and work. What Moses heard was beautiful, probably even profound, but . . . too much for him. He understood nothing, not one concept, not one word. And a new sadness overcame him; he felt useless, diminished. Suddenly, he heard a question a pupil was asking the rabbi:

— What proof do you have that your views on the subject are correct? That your opinion, and only yours, is correct?

And the master, Rabbi Akiba, replied:

— I have it from my Masters, who had it from theirs, who for their part claimed Moses as their teacher. What I am telling you is what Moses heard at Sinai.

Amused, and flattered too, Moses—the first Jewish author—was mollified. But something continued to trouble him. He again turned to God:

— I don't understand, said he. Since You have at Your disposal a sage such as he, a teacher such as he, why do You need me? Let him be Your messenger to transmit the Law of Israel to the people of Israel!

But God interrupted him:

— Moses, son of Amram, be quiet! This is how I envision things!

Satisfied or not, Moses submitted. He insisted no more. Yet, after a while he could not repress his curiosity:

— Tell me . . . What will happen to him, later?

And once again God made him turn around to show him the future. And Moses saw Rabbi Akiba at the hour of death. He saw his agony, his martyrdom at the hands of the Roman executioners. And in his astonishment and distress he cried out for the third time:

— I do not understand, Almighty! Is this justice? Is this the reward for studying Your Law? Do those who live by it deserve such a death?

And once again God cut him short:

— Be quiet, son of Amram! Such is My will! This is how I envision things!

And Moses kept a respectful silence, just as, centuries later, Rabbi Akiba remained silent on the day when he faced both death and eternity.

Another legend:

When Moses learned that his hour had come, he refused to accept it. He wanted to go on living—though he was old and tired of wandering and fighting and being constantly tormented by this unhappy and flighty people he was leading across the desert.

He put on sackcloth, covered himself with ashes and composed fifteen hundred prayers; then he drew a circle around himself and declared: I shall not move from here until the decree is revoked.

And once more his words shook the universe to its very foundation; heaven and earth, in panic, consulted one another. What was happening? Had God decided to put an end to His Creation?

Then there came to Moses' aid the five Books of the Law which bear his name; they pleaded with God to extend his life. But their intervention was unsuccessful.

Then the fire joined its efforts to theirs—in vain. And the sacred letters too were rejected. Even the Name of God was turned down by God; its intervention proved useless as well.

Then followed an amazing dialogue between God and Moses, in which the Creator tried to persuade His trusted servant to submit to His laws:

— You must die, Moses, otherwise the people will turn you into an idol.

— Don't you trust me? asked Moses. Have I not yet proved my worth? Have I not destroyed the Golden Calf?

God could have replied that He trusted Moses but not the others. Instead He chose to make His point by appealing to His prophet's common sense.

— Moses, he asked, who are you?

— The son of Amram, said Moses.

— Who was Amram?

— The son of Yitzhar, said Moses.

— Who was Yitzhar?

— The son of Kehat, said Moses.

— And Kehat, who was he?

— The son of Levi, said Moses.

— And Levi?

— The son of Jacob, son of Isaac, son of Abraham . . .

And thus he continued to the first man, Adam.

— Adam? said God. Where is Adam?

— Dead, answered Moses. Adam is dead.

— And Abraham? And Isaac? And Jacob?

— Dead, said Moses. They are all dead. And the others too. All dead.

— Yes, said God, your ancestors are dead. And you, you alone wish to live forever?

But Moses discovered in himself new gifts of rhetoric:

— Adam? he said. Adam stole. I did not. Abraham? Abraham had two sons, one of whom did not belong to Your people. That is equally true of Isaac. But not of me. Both my sons are children of Israel.

At this point God seems to have lost His patience:

— Moses, he said more abruptly, you killed an Egyptian. Who ordered you to kill him? Not I.

And once more Moses found an answer.

— Yes, I killed one single Egyptian. But You? You killed many. You killed all the first-borns. And You want to punish me?

Still, Moses knew that no matter how good his argument, it did not change the situation. The divine will reflects a divine and not a human logic. And so, in desperation, he turned to all of creation for help:

— Heaven and earth, pray for me!

— No, said they, we cannot.

Then he pleaded with the sun and the moon to pray for him.

— No, said they, we cannot.

Next came the stars, the planets, the mountains and rivers.

— No, they all said. We cannot even pray for ourselves.

Then Moses turned to the sea:

— You, please intercede in my favor!

And the sea, cruel and vindictive, reminded him of their first meeting, long ago, when he was leading a newly liberated people toward challenging adventures.

— Son of Amram, the sea sneered at Moses, what is the matter with you today? Now you need me? You who struck me with your stick and made me withdraw in order to let your people pass?

And Moses realized how alone and helpless he was. And ruefully he whispered—almost to himself:

— Once upon a time I was king and I gave orders; now I am on my knees and the whole world is indifferent.

Whereupon, in a surge of generosity, the illustrious Angel of the Face, the *Sar Hapanim Metatron,* gave him the friendly advice to stop opposing God's plan:

— I was present when the decision was taken and I heard, I heard them proclaim that the decree was sealed and could not, would not be suspended.

Moses should have heeded such knowledgeable and well-meaning advice; he should have left in a gracious, dignified manner. But he did not. He went on refusing to die, pleading, crying for another day, another hour, as would any common mortal—and not the prophet of prophets who had imposed his vision on mankind, the teacher of teachers who had felt God's fiery breath on his naked face!

So great was his despair that he declared himself ready to renounce his human condition in exchange for a few more days of life:

— Master of the Universe, he implored, let me live like an animal who feeds on grass, who drinks spring water and is content to watch the days come and go.

God refused. Man is not an animal; he must live as a human or not at all.

— Then, said Moses, permit me to stay here as a bird, friend of the wind, returning to his nest every night, grateful for the hours it has lived.

Again God said no. Man must live and die as a man, like all men.

Then God used a striking expression:

— Moses, you must die. You have already made too many words.

But Moses was still not resigned. He fought fiercely to the end, until abruptly, he appealed to death to come, as we shall see later.

The reader cannot help but be troubled by Moses' violent passion for life.

How could Moses, so zealous, so loyal, oppose the divine will? Or even question it? Is it not a privilege to die for God and His glory?

Why was he so anxious to continue living? After all, he was not exactly young, having reached the age of one hundred and twenty. Furthermore, had his life been so happy, so rewarding? He had constantly been tested and punished by God and man. No one had ever shown him any gratitude or even friendship. His people had made him suffer so much that he had begun to doubt himself and his mission. They had distorted his ideals, betrayed his trust; there had been few joys in his life. Why, then, did he cling to it so passionately instead of going quietly, serenely toward infinite peace?

And even if he did want to live so desperately, why did he show it? Why did he make such a display of his appetite for life? Was this behavior worthy of the founder and leader of a nation? Most great men, as we know, tend to conceal their feelings and suppress their anguish; they try hard to welcome death with contempt, or at least indifference. How, then, is one to explain that one of the most extraordinary figures in history behaved so oddly? Could he have "forgotten" Rabbi Akiba, appointed by God, who was to accept martyrdom silently and even joyfully?

Moses, the most solitary and most powerful hero in Biblical history. The immensity of his task and the scope of his experience command our admiration, our reverence, our awe. Moses, the man who changed the course of history all by himself; his emergence became the decisive turning point. After him, nothing was the same again.

It is not surprising that he occupies a special place in Jewish tradition. His passion for social justice, his struggle for national liberation, his triumphs and disappointments, his poetic inspiration, his gifts as a strategist and his organizational genius, his complex relationship with God and His people, his requirements and promises, his condemnations and blessings, his bursts of anger, his silences, his efforts to reconcile the law with compassion, authority with integrity—no individual, ever, anywhere, accomplished so much for so many people in so many different domains. His influence is boundless, it reverberates beyond time. The Law bears his name, the Talmud is but its commentary and Kabbala communicates only its silence.

Moshe Rabbénu, our Master Moses, incomparable, unequaled. The only man ever to have seen God face to face. Guide and supreme legislator. The Talmudic expression "Such is the law that Moses received at Sinai" inevitably leads to the closing of any debate. He is both source of every answer and root of every question. Every question that will ever be posed to a teacher by his pupil, Moses already heard at Sinai, says the Talmud.

Nevertheless, his portrait as sketched by tradition is carefully balanced; we are shown his shortcomings as well as his virtues. Unlike the founders of other religions or great leaders in other traditions, Moses is depicted as human, both great and fallible. While every other religion tends to transform its founder into a semi-god, Judaism does everything to humanize Moses.

Occasionally one even gets the impression that the Talmud would like to convince us that the greatest of our leaders was not really qualified to fulfill his duties; none of his failings are concealed, nor are his abrupt changes of mood. He did not get along well with other men or even with the angels. He married the daughter of a pagan priest, lived far away from his people and once even went so far as to deny his origins. Moreover, he was a poor speaker—how could he hope to galvanize his public?

And yet. Were it not for him, Israel would have remained a tribe of slaves. Living in the darkness of fear, dreading light.

His life began with tears, his own. Batya, the Pharaoh's daughter, noticed a basket floating down the Nile and discovered in it a Jewish infant—she knew it was Jewish because it cried not like an infant but like an adult, like a community of adults—his entire people was crying in him, said one of the commentators.

Legend tells us that Moses did not wish to cry. On the contrary, he tried to hold back his tears, to remain calm and silent though he was afraid. But the angel Gabriel struck him hard to make him cry so as to arouse Batya's pity. This may explain the tense relationships Moses was to have later with the angels.

When he was brought to the royal palace, Moses stopped crying. And soon began to dazzle the king and his court with his intelligence. He became the most spoiled of

183

children. And also the most precocious: at three years of age he displayed the gifts of a healer. And of a prophet. And since he was an exceptionally handsome child, people showered him with love. Batya, his adoptive mother, was constantly cajoling him. He was given all the advantages of the best education available; he studied with teachers from afar, stunning them with his industry and understanding. In hardly any time at all, he mastered several languages and the exact sciences. Pharaoh himself could not keep from covering the boy with signs of affection and often took him on his lap to play with him—an intimacy not without danger. One day, when the child playfully took the crown from the royal head and placed it on his own, the Pharaoh's counselors were dismayed; they called it high treason and the priests declared it a bad omen. All agreed that the child should be put to death before it was too late. Fortunately, one advisor—an angel in disguise—suggested a less radical solution. Set two plates before the child, one piled high with gold and precious stones, the other with burning coals: should the child reach for the gold, it would bear out that he indeed harbored suspicious intentions and that he had to be killed, but if instead he reached for the hot coals, then it would simply mean that he was attracted by shiny objects. This was done, and Moses indeed stretched out his hand to touch the gold and precious stones, but the angel Gabriel pushed him so hard that his hand seized a hot coal and brought it to his mouth. Thus Moses was saved—but his tongue was burned, and from then on he stuttered.

184

Thereafter he became more prudent and therefore more secure. Perhaps some of the royal advisors continued to suspect him, but we are not told about it. In fact, we are told nothing about his adolescence. Did he have any contact with his slave brothers? Was he aware of his origins? There is no mention of it either in the Bible or the Talmud. We are told only that one day *Vayigdal Moshe vayetze el echav—He grew up and went out to see his brethren.* (The Gerer Rebbe interprets this as meaning: Moses' greatness was that he went out to join his people.) How old was he then? Twenty, according to one source; forty, according to another. What is important is that he appeared among his brothers as a prince, with all the rights and privileges due his rank. An abyss separated him from the world of suffering. Yet the slaves' hunger and suffering did touch him; so much so that he decided to intervene.

The Midrash tells us that on that day Moses saw strong men carrying light burdens and weak men straining under heavy loads; old men performing the tasks of young men and young men doing work suited for old men; men assigned to do women's chores and women carrying out men's work. So shocked was Moses by this sight that he decided to intercede on their behalf and arrange that from that time on, everyone was assigned work according to his or her ability.

But Moses did not stop there. Once awakened, his sense of kinship with his people moved him to take further steps, involving more and more risks to himself. He improved their living conditions. He obtained for them the right to observe Shabbat, he took part in their internal affairs. In effect, he proclaimed himself protector of their interests.

One day, when he saw an Egyptian overseer torturing a slave, he threw himself on the man and killed him. From then on he spent all his time far from the palace, learning the mores and customs of these men and women persecuted by the powerful machinery of the empire. He wanted to understand, to help; to understand in order to be able to help more efficiently. He tried to comprehend the cruelty of the oppressors and that of some of the overseers chosen from the ranks of the slaves. Why did the victims, instead of helping one another, adopt the methods of their enemies? One day he saw two Jews quarreling. When one began to strike the other, he intervened. *Rasha,* he admonished the culprit, *you wicked man, why are you striking your brother?* In truth, it hardly seems to have been his business—why should an Egyptian prince care if two Jewish slaves felt like having a fight? But he already felt committed as a Jew and people were beginning to take notice. These two Jews knew. And so the man he had addressed answered insolently: Spare us your sermons; are you planning to kill us *too?* The man knew Moses' secret: that he had killed to save a Jew—and that he himself was Jewish. Otherwise he surely would not have dared to speak so rudely to one of the Pharaoh's favorite princes.

Denounced, betrayed, Moses had to flee. The Talmud tells us that an angel who resembled him like a brother gave himself up in his place, and that while he was facing the executioner, the real Moses escaped outside the country. Another source tells of another miracle: all the men at the royal court were stricken blind, deaf or mute; those who had seen or heard him leave could not speak of it. Another text has it that Moses was arrested by the Pharaoh's guards and condemned to have his head cut off, but that his neck miraculously resisted the ax.

What is certain is that this was a turning point for Moses, one of the most important in his life. It was not easy for a young man used to a princely life and the friendship of the great of this world to become a helpless fugitive overnight. Nor was it easy to break with his friends and habits and adapt himself to the life of a refugee.

When he accepted his new allegiance, Moses became a stranger in more ways than one: a stranger to the Egyptian people, to the Jewish people and to himself.

After many adventures the fugitive arrived in the land of Midian, where he settled, having found food and shelter and work as a shepherd. He married a native girl—the daughter of the priest Yitro. Two sons were born to them, Eliezer and Gershom, and they led a peaceful, idyllic existence, devoid of problems, dangers or conflicts. Did he sometimes remember his parents, his persecuted brethren? Apparently not. At least nothing in the texts or legends alludes to it. Their fate was no longer his concern. A vast desert separated him from them and he was content. Whatever was happening there, in faraway Egypt, no longer interested him. He took care of his family, of his flock, and that was enough for him to fill his time and justify his life as a man. Strange, for forty years Moses lived in his new adopted land without ever worrying about his family's fate. It seems unlikely somehow. What had taken place inside him? How is one to explain this sudden indifference? He who had risked his fortune, his freedom, his future to save one single life—why didn't he at least try to ascertain whether his people, an entire people, was still suffering or had been allowed some respite? This behavior does not fit in with Moses' temperament or with the logic of the events: to have opted for Judaism, at the price of a real sacrifice, only to give it up, just like that? It doesn't make sense.

There is one plausible explanation: Moses was disappointed in his Jews, and on several levels. They had not resisted, nor had they agreed to rebel. *Hasevel shesavlu bemitzraim*—They had settled into their "tolerance of suffering": resignation. (*Lisbol,* infinitive of *shesavlu,* means both to suffer and to tolerate.) He may have resented their inability to overcome their internal differences and unite against the enemy; there was too much pettiness, too much envy, too much selfishness. And then, too, they had betrayed him, their benefactor; for that there had been betrayal, he did not doubt. But who had been the informer? Well, let us see. When Moses killed the Egyptian overseer, who else had been present? Only one man: the very Jew whom Moses had saved.

For Moses this must have been a crushing experience—

with terrifying implications. Could he have come to the conclusion that the Jews were, after all, not worthy of the freedom he wanted for them? That they had fallen too low, had become too used to servitude to be redeemable? Could that have been the real reason why he had fled the country? Not because of Pharaoh, but because of the Jews? He probably could have soothed the king's anger. After all, the man he had killed was an obscure overseer and such a crime was not considered terribly serious in ancient Egypt. Surely Moses would have been forgiven. But his fear of Pharaoh was insignificant compared to his disillusionment with the Jews!

Let us follow this hypothesis further and we shall understand why, when he arrived in the land of Midian, he concealed his identity. They assumed he was Egyptian and he chose not to correct their mistake. He was a hidden Jew in search of assimilation, so much so that his second son was not circumcised. Moses, once more, was far removed from his people, though this time deliberately. Nothing is more painful than the sight of victims adopting the behavior and laws of their executioners. If the Jews behaved like the Egyptians, why should Moses be concerned with their fate? He preferred to forget them.

In this context, we can perhaps understand why, at first, he refused to serve as God's messenger. It took God seven days to convince him, says a Midrash. Moses refused, advancing all kinds of arguments: Why me? Why not an angel? Or my older brother Aaron? I am a poor speaker; also I am married and I have children; my father-in-law will object. And furthermore, what am I supposed to tell the Jews when they start asking me questions, so many questions? What shall I say? And what shall I tell the Pharaoh when *he* begins to ask me questions? Clearly Moses had no wish to return to his brothers, no wish to reopen a wound that had still not healed.

Yet in the end he gave in. God always wins. The last word is always His, as was the first.

Also, consider the setting: the flaming bush in the immensity of the desert; the all-pervasive solitude, the anxiety, the Voice both distant and close, insisting, probing, throbbing, burning. How could any human being, even Moses, resist that Voice indefinitely? And so Moses gathered his family, bid his in-laws farewell and set out on his return journey, albeit with noticeable lack of enthusiasm. That very night he stopped to sleep at an inn. Why not rest the night? And thus postpone the moment when he would meet once more those brothers he had expected never to see again? And what if by some chance he were to happen on his informer? At this point Moses would undoubtedly have preferred to die. That was why he did not resist the mysterious assault by an angel. His wife Tzipora saved him; her quick move to circumcise their son was meant to remind both God *and* Moses of the covenant: Moses could not die, must not die, not yet. Israel needed him—and so did God—and Israel could not, must not, die.

We can find what ensued in the Book of Exodus. Event followed event at a feverish pace. Leaving the calm of the desert, Moses plunged into the whirlpool of history. In

Egypt he witnessed and lets us witness the disintegration of an empire. Everything is falling apart and at dizzying speed. The participants in the drama are carried away by passions and unknown currents. The text becomes breathless, driven by an irresistible force. An epic poem with a thousand fragments joined in light. Everything is described in an intense, precise manner: the mood of the people, the fear of the slaves, the empty arrogance of the rulers, the calls to insurrection, the reverberations among the powerful as well as among the oppressed. What to do, what not to do? The first doubts on both sides, the first disagreements. Accept the challenge or submit. Tergiversations in the wretched huts as well as in the palaces darkened by malediction. What to do? What to say? Whom to follow? How was one to discern the signal of redemption, the sense of history?

At first Moses and his brother Aaron were alone, without allies or companions. Moses saw that his skepticism was justified: the slaves wanted to remain slaves. The Midrash tells us that on their arrival in Egypt, Moses and Aaron were welcomed by the Elders of the tribes of Israel, who declared themselves ready to follow them to the end. They set out for the royal palace, but gradually, as they came closer, the Elders changed their minds. With each step the group shrank. By the time they entered the Pharaoh's residence, the two brothers remained alone. If the Elders had lost their courage, if the leaders had succumbed to fear, what could one expect from the average Jew?

No, the slaves were not ready to leave—no more than the Pharaoh was ready to let them leave. Had the Pharaoh been particularly shrewd, he could have said: You want an exodus? With pleasure. I can do without all these Jewish slaves. So take them, and good riddance. But one question: Have you asked *them*—are you sure *they* want to leave? Fortunately, God kept the Pharaoh from playing that game, thus sparing Moses the humiliation of facing slaves reluctant to follow him. One text tells us that while Moses was negotiating the liberation of the Jews with the Pharaoh, Aaron was engaged in trying to convince the Jews to accept freedom. This earned him the honor of becoming the first high priest.

When the negotiations proved fruitless, other methods were tried; the curses, the plagues followed one another, yet without resembling one another. Here again, the text fairly bursts with descriptive power. It is as though one can hear the cries, the lamentations, the shouted orders, picked up and transmitted. The last night, the last chance. A number of non-Jewish slaves and Egyptians decided to join the movement: never again would they have such an opportunity to leave. One can almost hear the Egyptian parents mourning the death of their children, and Moses' lieutenants jostling and exhorting the people: Let's go, let's go, fast, faster. The race against time had started; it was late, later than was thought. The fleeing slaves had but one night to break the vise, to escape their prison. Tomorrow the oppressor would regroup his forces. Tomorrow he would regret his weakness. Tomorrow was at hand, tomorrow was here.

One could see people running, running breathlessly, without a glance backward; they were running toward the sea. And there they came to an abrupt halt: this was the end; death was there, waiting. The leaders of the group, urged on by Moses, pushed forward: Don't be afraid, go, into the water, into the water! Yet, according to one commentator, Moses suddenly ordered everyone to a halt: Wait a moment. Think, take a moment to reassess what it is you are doing. Enter the sea not as frightened fugitives but as free men! And everyone obeyed. They paused in their rush toward the sea. And Moses turned to God with a prayer. But God reminded him that this was not the right moment: Tell the people of Israel to hurry! And the people, united as never before, swept ahead and crossed the Red Sea, which drew back to let the Jews go through. And, we are told, so awesome and charged with faith was this sight that the most humble of servant girls saw in it more divine mysteries than the prophet Ezekiel perceived centuries later. And Moses began to sing. The stutterer, who could never utter a sentence longer than *Shlakh et ami*—Let my people go—composed the most majestic, the most lyrical poem in Scripture.

How did the stutterer turn into a minstrel? (Today we are told that while stutterers have difficulties in speaking, they have no problems in singing; this is probably true only since Moses.) The Hasidic explanation: *Vayaaminu baadoshem uv Moshe avdo*—And they had faith in God *and* in his servant Moses. For the first time an entire people rallied around Moses; for the first time he became its true spokesman. That was why he was able to sing; through him an entire people was singing.

Was this the moment of grace? The whole world became song. Even the angels began to sing, but God interrupted them with the most universally human call to order in the Talmud: *Maase yadai tovim bayam veatem omrim shira?*—My creatures are drowning in the sea—and you are singing? What if they are enemies of Israel and liberty—they are still human beings! How can you think of singing while human beings are drowning? Of course, the angels could have replied: What about the Jews, why is it all right for them to sing? The angels, perhaps out of politeness, did not ask the question. Besides, there *was* a difference: the Jews had just escaped disaster—the angels had not. As a surviving people, a people of survivors, Israel had the right—and duty—to express its gratitude.

Then, seven weeks later, came the big moment, the unique event in the memory of mankind: God was about to speak, to reveal His Law, to make His Voice heard. For three days the people and its leaders lived in expectation and purification; one must be worthy to receive the Law, worthy of being seen by God. Yet, if one is to believe Talmudic legend, there were those who were not impressed. On the morning of the day when all Israel was to have gathered at the foot of the mountain, some men and women were still asleep in their tents. And so God first manifested Himself with thunder and lightning in order to shake, to awaken those who were foolish enough to sleep while time and the heart of mankind opened to receive the call of Him who lends mystery to all things. Then, abruptly, there was silence. And in this silence a Voice was heard. God spoke. What did He speak of? His secret work, His eternally imperceptible intentions? No, He spoke of man's relationship to man, of one individual's duties toward others. At this unique moment God wished to deal with human relations rather than theology. No wonder His audience was recalcitrant; after all, why not steal in a society where everyone else does? Why not kill in a world steeped in violence? The Talmud states it explicitly: Israel refused the Torah until God threatened them: *Kafa alehem har kegigit*—He lifted a mountain and held it over the crowd. It was either the Torah or death. They had no choice, and so they accepted the Law against their will and God was satisfied at last.

But not Moses. Moses, in his candor, would have liked to see his people accept the Law freely. And to freely pledge allegiance to the God who had promised to watch over its fate. But he said nothing. Forty days later everything was forgotten, everything collapsed. Standing at the top of the mountain, the tablets of the Law in his arms, Moses perceived an unwonted noise from down below: his people were dancing, rejoicing, worshipping the Golden Calf.

So angry was Moses, says one Midrash, that he was ready to kill . . . his own brother, Aaron. His disappointment was boundless: forty days after the Revelation at Sinai—a Golden Calf! Despite the magnitude of the events, of the divine manifestations, the crossing of the Red Sea and the other miracles, something of this stiff-necked people had stayed behind in bondage in Egypt!

This may explain Moses' ambiguous relationship with his people—and God. He desperately wanted the adventure to be successful . . . and it was not easy. He found himself constantly wavering between ecstasy and despair; failures followed triumphs, he never knew what to expect from his people.

Moses' outbursts of anger, even his abdication are understandable. This people he had chosen never gave him anything but worries. There was no pleasing, no satisfying them. Forever complaining, grumbling, protesting, regretting the stability—however precarious, even miserable—of the past; the certainties—however debasing—of bondage. Moses' Jews showed no faith, no joy in being participants in the making of history.

No sooner had they left Egypt than they already asked to return: *Why did you make us leave?* They asked Moses: *Aren't there enough graves in Egypt? Why do you want to bury us all in the desert?*

Three days after the miraculous Red Sea crossing, all they wanted to know was: *Ma nishte?*—What is there to drink? Barely one month later they recalled Egypt with nostalgia: it was so good there; we ate all we wanted . . .

Even when Moses obtained the manna for them, they were not satisfied. At one point he became so exasperated that he cried out: *Oh, God, what am I to do with this ungrateful people? One more incident, and they will stone me to death!* On another occasion he had to remind them that he had taken nothing from them, that he had not become rich at their expense, and that he owed them nothing. One does not make such statements unless one stands accused.

Listen to a Midrash: Among the children of Israel, there were those who followed Moses with their eyes, saying: Look at this neck and look at that belly and those legs; whatever he eats, he has taken from the Jews; whatever he drinks, he has taken from the Jews; everything he owns comes from the Jews.

The line *And they were jealous of Moses* is commented upon by one text in a very explicit manner: every husband suspected him of engaging in illicit relations with his spouse. Everyone seems to have tried to pull him down to their own level.

Poor Moses, who had dreamed of inspiring them, elevating them, transforming slaves into princes, fashioning a community of free and sovereign men. Here was his dream—broken, shattered. The Jews, unchanged, were still absorbed in their sordid intrigues and in-fighting. They had seen God at work and had learned nothing. They had witnessed events of cosmic importance and had remained unaffected. *Hayesh adoshem bekirbenu im ayin?*

They were already doubting God's presence in their midst. They were already doubting their purpose, their very memory.

Moses had expected something else from this chosen people: another kind of vision, another kind of loyalty. After their liberation they should have lived proudly, as free men, not like a pack of fugitives. *Vayekhal Moshe*— And Moses prayed—is interpreted in the Midrash as: They made Moses sick. Too many people plaguing him with too many problems. We imagine him morose, unhappy. Only once do we see him joyous: on the day his brother Aaron acceded to the office of high priest. Otherwise he seemed far removed from happiness, and even more, from collective rejoicing. He was burdened with too many responsibilities, too much grief. He handled everything alone, without any help, without the benefit of comradeship and reliable allies. On the contrary, he felt that he was not liked; that the people mistrusted him, envied him. Here and there, young prophets plotted behind his back. Notables—from the Korakh clan—even prepared a coup to force him out of power. The scouts he had dispatched to the land of Canaan—famous people all—came back with disastrous reports that the Promised Land was inhabited by giants in whose eyes they had felt very small and frail. Two nephews—Aaron's sons—had penetrated into the sanctuary while in a state of drunkenness. His brother himself had had a hand in the making of the Golden Calf.

Things only got worse as time went on. One text tells

us that there were those who mocked him and treated him as if he were mad. Moses, the leader, the guide. When he presented the commandments to his people, he was interrupted by sneers: Are you going to lecture us, you stutterer? And: They took their children and threw them into his arms, shouting: Well, Moses, how are you going to feed them? What craft will you teach them? And: If he left his tent earlier than usual, they would ask: Why so early? If he left later than usual, they would ask: Why so late? If he left unnoticed, they would say: He is avoiding us, he is afraid of meeting us. Also: he explained the Law to them, but they refused to learn. After forty years of leadership, he still had to prove himself; every evening he had to tell them where they were and how many days had passed since Sinai. Only then were they prepared to admit that he was in full command of his mental faculties.

Who knows? Perhaps God's decision not to let him enter the promised land was meant as reward rather than as punishment.

A flighty, ungrateful people. Moses had good reason to despair, to castigate—and he did so often. Some commentators say: too often and too severely. And that was why he was punished. Yet if others spoke ill of Israel, he was quick to come to its defense, passionately, fiercely; there are times when Jews—and Jews alone—may criticize other Jews. Moses defended them not only against their enemies but, at times, even against God.

Says the Midrash: only by pleading for his people did Moses become an *Ish Elokhim,* a Man of God.

For, in fact, he filled two equally difficult roles: he was God's emissary to Israel and Israel's to God.

The moment the angels spoke out against Israel—and that happened frequently—Moses took its defense. When God decided to give His Law to Israel and the angels opposed His plan, Moses scolded them: Who then will observe it? You? Only man can assume the Law and live by its precepts.

And when his people sank to their lowest depths by dancing around the Golden Calf, Moses still found it possible to defend them: Whose fault is it, God, theirs or Yours? You let them live in exile, among idol-worshippers so long that they have been poisoned; is it their fault that they are still addicted? Then came his ultimatum: Either You forgive them everything or You erase my name from Your Book!

And when God said to him: *Ki shikhet amkha*—Your people have sinned—Moses replied with a sudden display of humor: When they observe Your Law, they are Your children, but when they violate it, they are mine?

Another time he remarked: Master of the Universe, do not get too angry, it is useless. Were You to destroy heaven and earth, Your people would survive—for that is what You pledged, remember? So why get angry?

In spite of his disappointments, in spite of his ordeals and the lack of gratitude he encountered, Moses never lost his faith in his people. Somehow he found both the strength and the courage to remain on Israel's side and proclaim its honor and its right to live.

All that he had been subjected to, all he had experienced notwithstanding, he knew how to accept every gift with gratitude. Moses was gratitude personified. Of his ten names, he retained that of Moses—because that was the name given to him by Batya, the Pharaoh's daughter; Batya who had saved his life.

When the great plagues befell Egypt, it was Aaron and not Moses who struck the Nile with his stick, transforming it into a river of blood. Moses would not do it, for he did not wish to harm the river that had saved his life.

Later, when Israel had to go and fight the nation of Midian, it was led by Joshua, not Moses; Moses would not fight his former adoptive country whose people had once given him shelter.

And now, let us return to our initial question: Why was Moses so attached to life, to the point of opposing God's will? Was that his way of protesting heaven's use of death to diminish, stimulate and ultimately crush man? Was it his final act on behalf of his people? His way of teaching Israel an urgent and timeless lesson: that life is sacred— always and for everyone—and that no one has the right to give it up? Did the most inspired and fierce prophet of all wish by his example to tell us, through centuries and generations to come, that to live as a man, as a Jew, means to say yes to life, to fight—even against the Almighty—

for every spark, for every breath of life?

Of course, it is also possible that Moses refusing to die is nothing but the image of a still vigorous old man afraid to die; the image of a human being, with human shortcomings and anxieties. As his last hour approached, he refused to act out the role of saint or hero; he wanted to live and admitted it. He had never lied, not to others and not to himself; he was not going to start now, on the threshold of death.

Yes, he wanted to live and was not ashamed of it; he wanted to live at any cost, except at someone else's expense. The Midrash tells us that at the end God told Moses: You insist on belonging to the world of the living, so be it, you shall live—but then Israel shall perish; it must be one or the other, you or Israel. And Moses cried out: Let Moses die, let a thousand men like him die, only let not one child of Israel be touched. For one may not go beyond a certain limit; to live is good, to want to live is human, but not at the expense of another's death.

Moses was a humanist in all things. Even his courage, his generosity were human virtues; all his qualities and all his flaws were human. He had no supernatural powers, no talent for the occult. Everything he did, he conceived in human terms, concerned not with his own "individual salvation" but with the well-being of the community. Once he reached heaven, he could have stayed there, but he chose to come back. He could have kept the truth he had just discovered to himself, but he chose to share it with the others. Though chosen by God, he refused to give up on man. Just as God brought Moses closer to man, Moses brought Him closer to man; he lived to share.

Another story underlines that vulnerability in him which is the reason each of us recognizes oneself in him. At the end of their seemingly interminable exchange, God consented to let Moses live, on condition that he accept having his disciple Joshua become his Master and that of the entire people. Moses agreed and immediately regretted it, exclaiming: Rather a thousand deaths than one moment of jealousy!

Moses was capable of jealousy; the prophet was human.

Let us now listen to how he died:

When Moses finally agreed to accept the inevitable, he begged God not to place him into the hands of the Angel of Death, who frightened him. And God promised. Three times did the Angel of Death move toward Moses, yet he was powerless to do anything but look at him from afar.

Moses spent his last hour blessing Israel's tribes. He began blessing them one by one, but time was running out and so he included them all in one benediction.

Then, escorted by the priest Eleazar and by his son Pinhas, and followed by his disciple Joshua, he began to climb Mount Nebo. Slowly he entered the cloud waiting for him. He took one step forward and turned around to look at the people following him with their gaze. He took another step forward and turned around to look at the men, the women and the children who were staying behind. Tears welled up into his eyes, he no longer could see anyone. When he reached the top of the mountain, he halted. You have one more minute, God warned him so as not to deprive him of his right to death. And Moses lay down. And God said: Close your eyes. And Moses closed his eyes. And God said: Fold your arms across your chest. And Moses folded his arms across his chest. Then, silently, God kissed his lips. And the soul of Moses found shelter in God's breath and was swept away into eternity.

At the foot of the mountain, shrouded in fog, the children of Israel wept. And all of creation wept. And in his sorrow, Joshua forgot three hundred commandments and acquired seven hundred doubts. And the bereaved people, blinded by grief, wanted to tear Joshua to pieces for having succeeded Moses, the saddest and loneliest and the most powerful prophet of Israel and the world.

But up above, the exulting angels and seraphim gave him a rousing welcome. Their joy reverberated throughout the celestial spheres. Everywhere Moses was celebrated as having been the most faithful of God's servants. The events that had filled his life on earth were glorified. Heaven glorified him seven times. And the waters glorified him seven times. And the fire glorified him seven times. And all of human history continues to glorify his name.

Nobody knows his resting place. The people of the mountains situate it in the valley. The people of the valley situate it in the mountains. It has become neither temple nor museum. It is everywhere and elsewhere, always elsewhere.

Nobody was present at his death. And so, in a way, he lives on inside us, every one of us. For as long as one child of Israel, somewhere, proclaims his Law and his truth, Moses lives on through him, in him, as does the burning bush, which consumes man's heart without consuming his faith.

PARABLES AND
SAYINGS VI

T*his is why and how God decided to put an abrupt end to the Jews' suffering in Egypt:*

In accordance with his desire to inflict pain on his slaves, Pharaoh issued orders to seize all male infants and wall them in alive inside the pyramids. And God stood by silently. The desperate parents cursed themselves for having brought children into the world. All the men and all the women agreed that they would not live together any more. And God stood by silently. Then one day an angel seized a newly born infant, who had already been tortured, already been disfigured, and held him up to God, who, grief-stricken, remembered the promise made to Abraham, Isaac and Jacob. That was when He set into motion the events which resulted in the Exodus: in those days God could not tolerate the sight of a mutilated Jewish child.

He made Moses His messenger. And the consoler of His people.

206

In the days when Moses was still a prince, he visited the slaves from morning till night, urging them not to lose courage.

He told them: Clouds are always followed by sunshine; after the storm comes the calm. Better days will come for us.

And God said to him: Just as you have left your palace to take care of Israel's children, your brethren, so shall I leave My celestial throne to speak with you.

In the land of Midian, Moses led the peaceful life of the shepherds.

One day he saw a sheep leave the flock; he pursued it until he found it drinking from a stream. And Moses said softly: I didn't know you were thirsty. You must be very tired after running so far; you don't have the strength to go back. And he lifted the sheep onto his shoulders and carried it back to the flock.

And God said to him: Since you have such great compassion toward this flock which belongs to a mortal, I shall entrust to you My own flock, the people of Israel.

Why did God choose to appear to Moses in a bush? To show His modesty: the bush is the smallest and most insignificant of trees.

And also to underline the symbolical aspect of the event: the bush is Israel. And just as the bird cannot penetrate the bush without getting caught on its thorns, the ene-

mies of Israel will not be able to harm it without being wounded.

The meeting between Moses and the Pharaoh was stormy, particularly since the king had been interrupted while dictating his correspondence to seventy scribes who formulated his letters in as many languages.

At the sight of Moses followed by his brother, the frightened scribes fell to their knees, letting their pens drop to the floor. The two brothers then challenged the Pharaoh: In the name of the God of Israel, we ask you to let our people go. The Pharaoh asked angrily: Who is this god you are referring to? What is his name? What does his power consist of? How many cities, how many provinces, how many countries have his legions occupied? How many wars has he won? Moses and Aaron tried to explain the inexplicable—that divine power has nothing to do with human ambition; it fills the universe and dominates the elements: it is He who every day decides who shall live and who shall die.

The Pharaoh asked to be brought the chronicles of all nations and sought in them the name of the God of Israel; he did find the names of the gods of Moab, and those of the gods of Sidon, and those of the gods of Ammon, but not that of the God of Israel. Moses and Aaron furnished him the reason: You are mad to seek the living in the graves of the dead. All these names of all these gods are names of dead gods, whereas our God is alive! Not to be persuaded, the

Pharaoh replied: Well, I don't know him and I shall not obey someone I do not know.

And so God made Himself known to Pharaoh. By punishing him.

At the foot of Sinai the freed slaves accepted the Law, and at that very moment one hundred and twenty myriads of angels descended from heaven and placed a crown on the head of every son of Israel. They were taken away later, when the people, in a moment of oblivion and impatience, begun to dance around the Golden Calf.

Were it not for this aberration, Israel would have remained a people of immortals; now it is only an immortal people.

That day was an ill-fated day for them in more than one way. God punished them by forcing them to study Torah not only in joy but in sorrow, not only as free men but in exile.

The return of the scouts, discouraged and discouraging, provoked such distress among the tribes that Moses decided to commemorate it every year.

At every anniversary Moses ordered the Jews to dig graves for themselves and to lie in them overnight. The next morning heralds ran between the trenches, shouting: Let the living separate from the dead, let the living detach themselves from the dead!

On the fortieth anniversary all rose, for by that time all of them belonged to the new generation; they were worthy of entering the Promised Land, for to them, bondage was no longer a temptation.

And the people of Israel mourned over Moses' death in the desert.
And sometimes, at night, the solitary pilgrim still hears their cries.

JOB: OUR
CONTEMPORARY

ONCE UPON A TIME, in a faraway land, there lived a man, just and wise, humble and charitable. His riches and his virtues aroused jealousy in heaven and on earth. His name was Job.

Through the problems he embodied and the trials he endured, he seems familiar—even contemporary. We know his history for having lived it. In times of stress it is to his words that we turn to express our anger, revolt or resignation. He belongs to our most intimate landscape, the most vulnerable part of our past.

Job: a moment of obsession, a gleam of anguish, a cry contained but not stifled trying to pierce our consciousness, a mirror a thousand times shattered reflecting the image of a solitude bursting with madness.

In him come together legend and truth; in him come together silence and the word. His truth is made of legends, his words are nourished by silence.

Whenever we attempt to tell our own story, we transmit

his. The opposite is true also: those of his legends we presumed invented, we lived through; those of his words we thought illusory, proved to be true; we owe them our experience of evil and death. In the midst of the blazing fire that ravages human forests, endowing them with ethereal beauty and mystery, we can but share his wonder.

In him we find the solitary conscience of Abraham, the fearful conscience of Isaac, the torn conscience of Jacob. Whenever the Midrash runs short of examples, it quotes Job, no matter what the topic—and it is always pertinent.

He reminds one of Abraham, for both their tragedies result from seemingly arbitrary ordeals. But unlike Abraham, he succeeded in maintaining a keen sense of humor. And unlike Abraham's, his story is *entirely* determined by legend, so much so that his very existence is placed in doubt by legend.

Let us begin again.

Once upon a time . . . When? Nobody knows. His name is mentioned by Ezekiel in passing, along with those of Noah and Daniel—was he a contemporary of one or the other? Possibly. Other legends link him alternately to Abraham, Jacob, Moses, Samson, Solomon, Ahasuerus and . . . the Babylonian exile. He would thus have lived not just two hundred and ten years but more than eight hundred.

Strange, he who knew no other land but his own—that of legend—seems to have lived in all of them; he who perhaps was never born, seems to have achieved immortality.

Understandably, he has fascinated innumerable storytellers and commentators through the centuries.

Records of his birth seem to proliferate. Though stateless, he belonged to more than one nation, to more than one era. He defies geography and chronology. Was he Jewish—this first world citizen? Possibly, though it is far from certain. More than likely he was not; many texts stress his character traits, his good deeds which make him into a Just Man or a prophet "among the Gentiles." Only a small minority insists on making him Jewish—an insistence based on the premise that a personality of his stature could be nothing else.

He is alternately described as a high Egyptian official, an advisor at the Pharaoh's court, a colleague of Balaam and Yethro. When the Pharaoh wondered how to resolve his own Jewish question, Yethro declared himself in favor of granting Moses' request—to let his people go—while Balaam opposed it. When consulted in turn, Job refused to take a stand, preferring to remain neutral, silent—neither for nor against. And it was for this neutrality, this silence, the Midrash tells us, that he incurred his later sufferings. In times of crisis, of danger, no one has the right to choose caution, abstention; when the life and death of a human community are at stake, neutrality becomes criminal.

One may suppose that this legend was invented to justify Job's subsequent ordeals; just as there is no crime without punishment, ideally there is no punishment without crime.

This seems a flawed explanation. How could Job be accused of indifference toward the persecuted Jews if he himself was not Jewish? Answer: Even if he was not a Jew by birth, he was one by adoption—a kind of honorary Jew. Related to Jews and close to them. One source claims that he was married to Dinah, Jacob's daughter.

One apocryphal work, "Job's Testament," goes further and says that he was Esau's son, which would make Dinah his cousin. And how did he succeed in entering Egypt's royal palace? His other cousin—Joseph—must have lent his support. As long as Joseph remained in power, Job was safe. His position must have weakened in the days when Moses began to make trouble. This would explain why he dared not express an opinion during the debate on the liberation of the Jews, preferring not to take part in that decision. A guilty, cowardly attitude for which he deserved punishment.

All of this is denied by another legend which describes him as solidly established in the land of Canaan, where he had settled long before the Jews' arrival. In fact, he died there on the very day Moses' scouts made their appearance. That was why they found the place so dull and deserted: its inhabitants were away attending the funeral of their prince, the illustrious Job. Thus it appears that the scouts were unjustly accused and punished; they had neither slandered nor defamed the Promised Land; they had described precisely what they had seen: deserted streets, abandoned homes, people in tears. It had been Job's fault; he should have chosen another time and place to die.

What is strange is that Moses was not informed. Was he not a prophet, and the greatest of all? Didn't he know that it would have been better to delay the scouts' departure? To have sent them out earlier or later? Moreover, isn't he supposed to be the author of the Book of Job (though it was written without divine inspiration)? He should have been well versed in the subject. In his defense we must note that Job is not an easy character to deal with: he was everywhere and everything at the same time. One might call him a hero in search of identity. As though his peregrinations through provinces and centuries were not enough to confuse us, there was also this Rabbi Shmuel, son of Nahman, who asserts that Job simply never lived, that he was only a symbol, a fable. Having said this, we have still not run out of surprises. The concept of poetic fiction encompasses the entire range of theories. There were those who claimed that Job did exist but that his sufferings are sheer literary invention. Then there were those who declared that while Job never existed, he undeniably did suffer.

Let us speak for a moment of this suffering without which his life would have been quite ordinary. Who doesn't remember the story? At the outset Job appears like a man fulfilled: wealthy, hospitable, influential, enjoying an excellent reputation at home and abroad. Whatever he possessed, he had acquired honestly. His house, open on all four sides so that every beggar passing through town could enter immediately and satisfy his hunger, recalled that of Abraham. The poor nomads of the Uz region knew only Job, visited nobody's house but his. As a center of hospitality and of attraction it was unique; people flocked to it from everywhere. Job never sent anyone away, never refused anything. And he gave without humiliating, he gave by giving of himself; nothing pleased him more. There was no sick person he didn't try to heal, no widow he didn't attempt to console. He spent his time helping the needy, those less fortunate than himself.

Was he happy? He never complained, true: he had nothing to complain about. He had a wife, seven sons, three daughters and an estate as huge as a kingdom. So busy was he dispensing his good deeds, so taken was he with his civic activities, that he somewhat neglected his children's education; they indulged in so many revelries that he eventually had to plead for pardon on their behalf.

All this we know from the Midrash and from the Book of Job itself, which Rabbi Yohanan could not read without weeping, for in it he came up against the eternal problem of immanent and transcendent justice on a human scale: Job, friend of man, tested by God, did not deserve his punishment.

The Book's prologue describes his dramatic downfall—a downfall startling in its speed; in no time at all, he lost his fortune, his possessions, his children, his friends, all his reasons to live. Disasters and tragedies followed in rapid succession. One after the other, messengers appeared, presenting brief, factual reports, pushing him gradually, systematically, into his role of hapless victim drawn into the abyss. The description is powerful, sober and realistic; the pace breathtaking. Messenger followed messenger, one arriving while the previous one was still making his report: Fire fell from the sky and burned cattle and shepherds alike; I am the only survivor, the only witness come to tell you the tale. And also: Your sons and daughters were eating and drinking in the house of your first-born when a terrible wind swept in from the desert, smashing the house, which collapsed, and all those in it were killed; I am the only survivor and only I can tell you the tale.

Job asked no questions, not even of himself. He never doubted the veracity of the reports. The thought that so many disasters could not possibly befall one home in such rapid succession did not enter his mind; he did not seek refuge in doubt. He believed. He accepted. He *knew* that the messengers did not lie. And acted accordingly.

He tore his clothes, cut his hair in token of mourning —but he did not complain, nor did he protest. He fell sick, his condition grew worse and worse until his entire body was covered with blisters and sores, horrible to see; yet he still did not complain. When his wife incited him to blasphemy, he refused to listen. (The Midrash generously paints a more attractive picture of his wife, describing her as having sacrificed herself to care for him with selfless devotion.) His dearest, closest friends came to visit him, pretending to console him. They were the ones who made

ELIE WIESEL

him lose his illusions about divine justice and human friendship. For the first time he opened his mouth to speak. And uttered his cry of malediction: May the day of my birth be lost in darkness, may the night that saw me be born remain mute and solitary. And then, in desperation, he asked the eternal question of the persecuted: Why? Why me? Why now? What is the meaning of punishment inflicted on a Just Man? What is God doing, and where is His justice?

Job knew, as we know, that he had committed no sin; he had nothing to reproach himself for, neither did God. Job knew, as we know, that all his life he had acted in accordance with God's will, fearing and loving Him, never violating a law, never transgressing a commandment. As a matter of fact, one finds nothing but praise and compliments about him in Midrashic texts. Some even go so far as to compare him to the greatest of our ancestors: Four men discovered God on their own—Abraham, King Ezechias, Job and the Messiah . . . What has not been said about Job? That he was born circumcised; that in his lifetime he tasted the fruits and pleasures of paradise. A Just Man among the Gentiles, he was reputed to have tried to save mankind through his suffering. Job: a different Messiah, working for the redemption of the Gentiles. Uncommon powers were ascribed to him. The alms he distributed became instruments and sources of benediction: whoever received a coin from him became rich. Job, a miracle-maker? Why not.

A Midrash tells us that in Job's kingdom the laws of

nature obeyed his will; the weak were not subjugated by the strong; the sheep dominated the wolves. King Solomon included him among the Seven Fathers of mankind. He almost entered our prayers. One of our sages tells us that had it not been for his anger, we would be invoking the God of Abraham, Isaac, Jacob *and* Job. We would be appealing to him, to him too, to intercede up there, to prevent God from turning away from His people.

But then, why was he punished? Prophet, judge, friend of the deprived, protector of orphans—what had he done to deserve so terrible a fate? To what, to whom, should one attribute his torments?

These questions preoccupied the Talmud before the tale of Job, for the "case Job" predates Job. Abraham had not sinned and yet he was tested. The parallel with Abraham seems deliberate; it reappears frequently. Both were kind and charitable men; both suffered. In their quarrels with God, they used almost identical language. Abraham questioned His justice with regard to Sodom and Gomorrah, Job with regard to himself. Abraham pleaded for a community of men, an entire city, Job pleaded for himself. Abraham's purpose was to prevent, Job's was to indict. And that is the key difference between the two. Abraham challenged God while defending someone else's interests, Job spoke out against injustice only when it affected him personally. Was that a reason to punish him?

The parallel between the two may have been meant as a consolation. The Midrashic commentators seem to be saying to Job: What are you complaining about? Your case is not unique. Do you think you are the only one whom God has made to tremble? There exists at least one precedent; what is happening to you has happened before and to someone greater than you: Abraham. And *he* submitted to God's will . . . A simplistic consolation, yet one that often works; the patient is reassured, or thinks he is, upon discovering that he is not the only one afflicted. Still, Job could have answered that he didn't care whether his case was new or not, for it in no way altered the question. Repetition of an offense is no excuse; evil is a personal experience for every individual, and to exorcise it, each must fashion his own weapons lest he go mad. Job could also have said that while the tragedy of one man may well be linked to that of another, or many others, that fact explains nothing and surely justifies nothing . . . But Job kept silent. He refuted nothing. It is the Midrash which reasons thus in his stead.

A story: When Rabbi Yohanan, son of Zakkai, lost his son, his disciples tried to console him. Rabbi Eliezer reminded him that the same tragedy had struck Adam, who knew how to overcome his grief. But Rabbi Yohanan, son of Zakkai, replied: Is my own grief not enough? Must you add Adam's? Then Rabbi Yehoshua reminded him of the ordeals endured by Job, who allowed himself to be consoled. But Rabbi Yohanan, son of Zakkai, replied: Is my own sorrow not great enough? Why do you wish to add that of Job? Then Rabbi Yossi reminded him of Aaron the high priest who witnessed the death of his two sons and knew how to contain his grief and remain silent. And Rabbi Yohanan, son of Zakkai, replied: Is my own anguish not deep enough? Must you add that of Aaron?

No, tragedies do not cancel each other out as they succeed one another. On the contrary, they multiply and accumulate, becoming more unjust with every blow. True, every man suffers alone—yet his suffering is never limited to himself. Suffering begets suffering ever sharper, deeper and more harrowing. In other words, Job's anguish, however similar to Abraham's, however reminiscent of Abraham's, cannot be explained by it. The fact that Job's torments had a precedent does not imply that they have a meaning. In this respect, Jewish tradition differs from the Buddhist concept: to insert individual anguish into cosmic anguish does not resolve, but on the contrary, aggravates the problem. Therein lies its universality. Every individual is both beginning and end; that is why he deserves an answer, not a consolation, unless the consolation itself becomes an answer.

One attempt at an answer is provided by the Book of Job, right at the beginning, in the sixth verse. We at once learn the name of the culprit: Satan, one of the *bnei Elokhim,* God's children, who takes a particular interest in human affairs. God is described as listening to Satan's travel impressions.

The eternal instigator of man against God is shown here

in the role of instigator of God against man. He challenged Him, and Job's faith became both instrument and stake of that challenge.

Job: a battlefield, a living example, a subject for debate, with immeasurable and, surprisingly, unforeseeable repercussions.

The dialogue between God and Satan was friendly at first, almost casual: Did you happen to see My good servant Job? Is he not the most pure and loyal of men? — Why wouldn't he be? came Satan's retort; he is good because You are good with him; he is charitable because You are charitable with him. He has everything he wants. Try shaking him, making him suffer, and we shall see his true face . . . And thus Job became the object of a superhuman, inhuman contest, the protagonist in a drama whose rules and points of reference he did not know and could not comprehend. He did not, he could not, understand what was happening to and around him. He was being pulled and pushed in all directions and he did not know that it was all part of a plan. At first he wondered whether his was not a case of mistaken identity, of terrible misunderstanding.

A legend: More in bewilderment than in sorrow, Job turned to God: Master of the Universe, is it possible that a storm passed before You causing You to confuse *Iyov* [Job] with *Oyev* [Enemy]?

Strange as it may seem, of all the questions raised by Job, only this one was answered. And God's voice roared in the tempest: Pull yourself together, man, and listen!

2 2 2

Many hairs have I created on the human head, and every single hair has its root; I don't confuse roots, how could I confuse *Iyov* and *Oyev?* Many drops have I created in the clouds, and every single drop has its own source; I confuse neither drops nor clouds, how could I confuse *Iyov* and *Oyev?* Many thunderbolts have I created and for each bolt a path of its own; I don't mistake one bolt for another, how could I confuse *Iyov* and *Oyev?* Know also that the wild goat is cruel with its young. As they are about to be born she climbs to the top of a very high rock and lets the little ones drop from the precipice. So I prepared an eagle to catch them on his wings, but were the eagle to arrive one moment too early or too late, they would fall to the ground and be crushed. I don't confuse moments, or lightning bolts, or drops, or roots—and you are asking Me if I am confusing *Iyov* and *Oyev,* Job and Enemy!

Was Job really so naïve as to suggest that God's vocabulary was faulty? His very question constituted a provocation. With his undoubtedly uncalled-for insolence, he wanted to irritate God, to force Him to justify His actions even retroactively. Since punishment there was, let it at least have some basis, some motivation. He wanted it to be a result, a consequence rather than a gratuitous act. In other words, Job would have preferred to think of himself as guilty. His innocence troubled him, left him in the dark; his guilt might give the experience a meaning. He would gladly have sacrificed his soul for knowledge. What he demanded was neither happiness nor reparations, but an answer, an answer that would show him unequivocally that man is not a toy, and that he is defined only in relation to himself. That was why Job turned against God: to find and confront Him. He defied Him to come closer to him. He wanted to hear His voice, even though he knew he would be condemned. He preferred a cruel and unjust God to an indifferent God.

Moreover, Job needed God because he felt abandoned by man. His wife was pushing him to the solution of the weak: resignation, denial, abdication. His friends had nothing to offer him except their pity, their incredulity. They were willing to concede that he was indeed suffering, but rather less than was apparent. They felt that he was wrong to react so intensely and wrong to wallow in his sorrow. Did he suddenly realize that he would never be able to communicate to them the enormity of his grief? He rebelled against those who refused to listen to the end, to look all the way, just as he stood up against this God in whose name his friends claimed to lie. On a deeply human plane, his revolt ultimately was directed against his own solitude, which he knew to be irreducible, for it concealed God's face beneath that of man.

There is no need to embellish the scene: it is described in the Book and illustrated in the Midrash in masterly fashion.

As the two celestial players withdrew backstage, Job received the visit of three of his friends: Elifaz the Yemenite, Bildad of Shukh, Tzofer of Naamat.

At first glance they did not recognize him: he had changed, they had not. Then they burst into tears, tore their garments, covered their foreheads with ashes, sat down beside him on the ground and did not open their mouths for seven days and seven nights. (In "Job's Testament," quoted earlier, his friends did not remain silent but questioned him a whole week on what had happened.) Says a Midrash: In deference toward the mourner, one imitates his behavior. Job's visitors rose when he rose, ate when he ate, drank when he drank. Without ever uttering a word, for certain griefs beget a silence that is commensurate to them; words could only betray them. We are moved by the three silent friends, but the moment they begin to speak they disappoint. Talkative. Hypocritical. Their emotions seem false, calculated. They had to choose between taking a stand for their beaten and defeated friend or for God. They made the wrong choice, the easiest one. These three self-righteous strangers from afar exaggerated when they tried to explain to Job events whose tragic weight rested only on his shoulders. *He* suffered, and *they* made speeches on suffering. *He* was crushed by sorrow, and *they* built theories and systems on the subjects of grief, suffering and persecution.

Said Elifaz: No man is without sin, yourself included. Who knows what you have done to attract the wrath of God.

Bildad tried gentleness: All right, I am willing to believe that you are innocent, but you must admit that God does

2 2 5

not make mistakes. Even if you yourself don't know what you have done, God surely knows.

The third, Tzofer, used the occasion to reproach him for his vanity: Who are you to question the ways and intentions of the Almighty? Do you think you can do whatever you wish just because you are God's victim?

Exasperated with his friends, Job chose to turn toward and against God. Understandably so: better to deal with God than with His commentators.

We can also understand why, in the Midrash, Job is compared to the Jewish people. Israel too is alone; its best friends are ready to commiserate in its misfortunes but will do nothing to help. Israel too has been accused of acting against God, forcing Him to resort to punishment. Israel too maintains an endless dialogue with God or on God. Israel too is persecuted by men who, after inflicting pain, denounce its people for attempting to bear suffering in a proud and dignified way. If Job was not Jewish to begin with, he became Jewish. There was no way he could win in a society where friendship was nonexistent and where to suffer and to expiate had the same meaning.

Some of our sages, emulating his three "friends," tried to console Job by reducing his problem to ordinary dimensions. A motive, a sin, had to be invented at all costs—why use restraint? Some accused him of lack of faith in the resurrection of the dead; others of arrogance and bad temper. *Iyov lokeh umevaet,* Job balked too much against his pain. Minor sins with disproportionate consequences. No, there had to be a better answer. And anyway, why speak of sin? One Midrash pictured him as martyr of the Jewish people.

Listen: When the children of Israel were about to leave Egypt, Satan rushed to God, protesting: Master of the Universe, think! Only yesterday these men and women were infidels, idol-worshippers, and You plan to perform miracles on their behalf? Are You really going to make them cross the Red Sea? And give them Your Law? Do You really trust them? In order to get rid of him, God pointed to Job and said: Go and take care of him first, we'll talk later. And while Satan was busy torturing his victim, God managed to free His people from bondage.

This concept is illustrated in the Midrash by the following parable: Imagine a shepherd who sees a wolf getting ready to jump on his flock—what does he do? He pits him against the strongest and fiercest of his rams, and while the wolf is locked in struggle with the ram, the shepherd ushers the rest of his flock to safety.

Logically, both Job and Satan had every reason to become anti-Semites: the Jews had taken advantage of them and the God of the Jews had tricked them.

While Job could console himself that at least he did not suffer in vain, Satan, who had made him suffer, remained inconsolable. Therefore, says one of the sages, Satan is more to be pitied than Job. Deceived by God, he found himself in the intolerable position of someone who must break the wine casket and save the wine; he was allowed to torture Job up to a clearly defined limit, yet Job was not to succumb; God wanted him alive.

Another text, more cruel toward Satan, denied his paternity of the project. According to that version, Job himself had chosen his role. God had asked him: Between poverty and illness, what would you choose? To which Job is said to have answered: I would rather suffer than live in deprivation. Though he appeared to be the grand master of the game, Satan was in fact only an instrument. Disgusted, he vanished from the scene. For good. Thereafter, he is not mentioned again in the Book of Job. His hurried departure led one sage to reintroduce him in the guise of a fourth friend, Elihu. Appearing unexpectedly, almost at the end, Elihu tried to drive Job to despair and, once again, failed. For Satan, one more failure. Poor Satan, disguised as friend, suddenly he is used by Midrashic legend in an attempt at black humor.

The great pages that follow the prologue need few imaginary tales; they would be superfluous. The text suffices to let us participate in the drama. The dialogues between Job and his friends, and later between Job and God, are of striking clarity. Eternal questions, poignant replies. Heaven and earth provide the setting for man's ultimate confrontation with himself and with his idea of God.

Listen to Job speaking: Granted, I am guilty, but why should that matter to You? In what way are You concerned by my deeds? And why did You designate me, who feel crushed by my own burden, as target? Are You pleased now, pleased to have opposed Your creation? I have garbed my body in sackcloth, I have rolled my head in ashes. My face is swollen from weeping and the shadow of death weighs on my brow . . . And then this outcry which, from generation to generation, through pogroms and massacres, reverberates from one end of exile to the other: *Eretz al tekhasi dami*—Earth, do not absorb my blood! Nature, do not shelter my despair! Job had nothing left in this world except words, but he knew how to use them; he made them quiver, he made them scream.

Up to that moment Job had been seeking support, a vantage point, but could not find them; he had been seeking someone to speak to—judge or avenger—and could find no such person. That was when the poorest, the most solitary man on earth—for he had possessed everything and lost everything—suddenly acquired unsuspected strength and decided to express his rebellion, deriving his courage and arguments from his very poverty, weakness and solitude. He rejected all easy solutions, all debasing compromises. He discovered within himself unequaled power and he reversed the roles. Though accused, condemned and repudiated, he defied the system that kept him imprisoned. He launched an inquiry and suddenly God was the defendant. Job spoke his outrage, his grief; he told God what He should have known for a long time, perhaps since always, that something was amiss in His universe. The just were punished for no reason, the criminal rewarded for no reason. The just and the wicked were subjected to the same fate—God having turned His back on them, on everyone. God had lost interest in His creation; He was absent.

Carried away by the passion of his indictment, Job ignored all taboos, overturned all obstacles. Freed of his inhibitions, he went far, too far. Through his so-called friends, whom he unmasked, he was aiming for God, his true adversary. Said Job: Whoever pleads with heaven becomes everybody's laughingstock. God despises the wretched. He who is so powerful and so just pushes away those who waver, while thieves rest in peace under their tents and those who deny God are without cares. Facing his visitors, Job cried out: Be quiet, I am going to speak, come what may. It is dangerous? No matter. I shall be killed? No matter. It is hopeless, I know, but I must speak . . . And later: I lift my eyes to God, crying that He may render justice to man who argues with Him.

This desperate act of courage was not futile. Abruptly God entered the tale and chose to make Himself heard. Says the Midrash: Job felt his hair caught in the tempest and that was when he heard the divine voice. Does this mean that the exchange took place only in his mind? Possibly. Actually, it makes no difference. Reality or delirium, Job felt that he had won. God was answering him. With a series of questions.

Listen to God speaking: Where were you when I created the mountains and the winds? What do you know of My secrets to dare question My means and My ends? What do you know about justice and the ways I choose to dispense it? And truth and good and evil, what do you know about them to dare defy Me?

Actually, God said nothing that Job could interpret as an answer or an explanation or a justification of his ordeals. God did not say: You sinned, you did wrong. Nor did He admit His own error. He dealt in generalities, offering nothing but vast simplifications. Job's individual experience, his personal misfortunes mattered little; what mattered was the context, the overall picture. The concept of suffering was more important than suffering; the question of knowledge was more important than knowledge. God spoke to Job of everything except that which concerned him; He denied him his right to individuality.

And yet, instead of becoming indignant, Job declared himself satisfied. Vindicated. Rehabilitated. He asked for nothing more; as far as he was concerned, justice had been done. The fierce rebel, the fighter who dared to face God and speak up as a free man, abruptly bowed his head and gave in. No sooner had God spoken than Job repented. Was he so proud of having inspired the divine poem, so satisfied to have heard God's voice, that he forgot both content and principle? Was he so impressed with the celestial voice that he forgot his resolution? No sooner had God finished His sermon than Job pulled back and withdrew his questions, canceled his complaints. Said he: Yes, I am indeed small, insignificant; I had no right to speak, I am unworthy of Your words and thoughts. I didn't know, I didn't understand. I couldn't know. From now on I shall live with remorse, in dust and ashes.

And so, there was Job, our hero, our standard-bearer, a broken, defeated man. On his knees, having surrendered unconditionally. God magnanimously allowed him to stand up again. And live again.

All is well that ends well; everybody was satisfied. Job, because he had heard God's voice. God, because Satan and Job had ceased to annoy Him. The three visitors, because Job seemed not to bear them a grudge. Only Satan could have felt wronged, but he was absent, definitively cast into oblivion.

As for the concrete aspect of his vindication, Job recovered his fortune, he even collected damages. He accumulated more riches, more glory than he had had before. He was happier than ever. He—again—became the father of seven sons and three daughters (the most beautiful in the world, says the Midrash) and lived another hundred and forty years. The last line in the Book is also the last stroke of irony: *Vayamat Iyov zaken useva yamim*—And Job died an old man, saturated with years. This can be interpreted as: Saturated with life; he had had enough. In spite of his apparent happiness, in spite of his regained wealth, he no longer cared to live. He now knew that it takes no more than idle talk, or a wager between strangers, for a human life to collapse like a sand castle in a storm.

Yet, when taken literally, these words could indicate that Job, once his ordeals were behind him, lived in peace with his destiny, reconciled with God and mankind.

And that is the point at which I register my protest. Much as I admired Job's passionate rebellion, I am deeply troubled by his hasty abdication. He appeared to me more human when he was cursed and grief-stricken, more dignified than after he rebuilt his lavish residences under the sign of his newly found faith in divine glory and mercy.

Many scholars disclaim the ending, insisting that it was added on, grafted onto the original Book in order to reassure devout believers. Or to teach persecuted men everywhere that man must be capable of losing everything without giving up hope. Like Job, one should be able to experience misfortune and nevertheless, at the first respite, take root again and give life. I prefer to think that the Book's true ending was lost. That Job died without having repented, without having humiliated himself; that he succumbed to his grief an uncompromising and whole man. It seems rather odd that the Midrash, so prodigal in legends at the beginning of the drama, becomes so sparing in its epilogue; it probably troubled the rabbinical storytellers. The third act of a play is usually a kind of apotheosis; this one is pale, disappointing. The fighter has turned into a lamb. A sad metamorphosis, inexplicable in literary terms.

And then, why not say it? I was preoccupied with Job, especially in the early years after the war. In those days he could be seen on every road of Europe. Wounded,

233

robbed, mutilated. Certainly not happy. Nor resigned.

I was offended by his surrender in the text. Job's resignation as man was an insult to man. He should not have given in so easily. He should have continued to protest, to refuse the handouts. He should have said to God: Very well, I forgive You, I forgive You to the extent of my sorrow, my anguish. But what about my dead children, do they forgive You? What right have I to speak on their behalf? Do I have the moral, the human right to accept an ending, a solution to this story, in which they have played roles that You imposed on them, not because of them, but because of me? By accepting Your inequities, do I not become Your accomplice? Now it is my turn to choose between You and my children, and I refuse to repudiate them. I demand that justice be done to them, if not to me, and that the trial continue . . . Yes, that is what he should have said. Only he did not. He agreed to go back to living as before. Therein lay God's true victory: He forced Job to welcome happiness. After the catastrophe Job lived happily in spite of himself.

At the end of his struggle, which Job recognized as being lost in advance—for how can man hope to defeat God?—Job discovered a novel method to persevere in his resistance: he pretended to abdicate before he even engaged his battle.

Had he remained firm, had he discussed the divine arguments point by point, one would conclude that he had to concede defeat in the face of his interlocutor's rhetorical superiority. But he said yes to God, immediately. He did not hesitate or procrastinate, nor did he point out the slightest contradiction. Therefore we know that in spite or perhaps because of appearances, Job continued to interrogate God. By repenting sins he did not commit, by justifying a sorrow he did not deserve, he communicates to us that he did not believe in his own confessions; they were nothing but decoys. Job personified man's eternal quest for justice and truth—he did not choose resignation. Thus he did not suffer in vain; thanks to him, we know that it is given to man to transform divine injustice into human justice and compassion.

Once upon a time, in a faraway land, there lived a legendary man, a just and generous man who, in his solitude and despair, found the courage to stand up to God. And to force Him to look at His creation. And to speak to those men who sometimes succeed, in spite of Him and of themselves, in achieving triumphs over Him, triumphs that are grave and disquieting.

What remains of Job? A fable? A shadow? Not even the shadow of a shadow. An example, perhaps.

Mishna
Talmud Bavli
Talmud Yerushalmi
Avot d'rabbi Nathan
Midrash Rabba
Midrash Tankhuma
Midrash Tehilim
Pirkei d'rabbi Eliezer
Divrei hayamim shel Moshe Rabenu (Venice, 1544)
The Testament of Job (Berlin, 1897)
Legends of the Bible, by Louis Ginzburg (Jewish
    Publication Society, 1972)
The Last Trial, by Shalom Spiegel (Pantheon, 1967)
L'Existence Juive, by André Neher (Seuil, 1962)
L'Exil de la Parole, by André Neher (Seuil, 1972)
Moses, by David Daiches (Praeger, 1975)

The main chapters in this volume are based on lectures deliv-
ered at the Sorbonne, the 92nd Street "Y," and at Stanford,
Hofstra and Brandeis Universities.

Messengers of God is the second volume in an overall series
which began with *Souls on Fire.*

ABOUT THE AUTHOR

ELIE WIESEL was born in 1928 in the town of Sighet in Transylvania. He was still a child when he was taken from his home and sent to Auschwitz and Buchenwald. After the war he was brought to Paris, where he studied at the Sorbonne. He has been an American citizen for some years, and he and his wife and family live in New York City. Besides writing and lecturing, he teaches at City College, where he holds the position of Distinguished Professor of Jewish Studies.